This Journal Belongs To:

Dressage Rider's Essential Notebook

ISBN: 9781693721816

Cover Image: Used under license by Canva Pro
Piaffe horse graphic by Stacie Campuzano

For more information go to
www.campuzanoequestrian.com

Instagram: @piaffedreams

Table of Contents

Show us your notebook on IG #dressagenotebook
Follow Stacie @Piaffedreams for more patterns to ride and more lesson notes.

Like on Facebook @CampuzanoEquestrian

Instructor: Date:

Keywords/Visuals	Notes
In this section, write quick word or phrase that triggers a visual, a feeling, or change that makes an improvement. Example: "Heavy elbows" "breathe"	What happened in your lesson? What were you working on? What were you trying to learn or train? Be sure to diagram the figures and geometry on the page to the right. But here is a good place to recognize the flow, how things felt, what things you want to remember. Pull out key phrases and quick visuals for recall to put in the box to the left.

Lesson Highlights

Every lesson has an ah-ha moment, something that went well. Write it here. Build on success. There's plenty of room for what needs improving.

Write a few tags for the content of the lesson. Go to your index and put the topics in the left column and the page # on the right.

20 x 60 Meter Dressage Court Dimensions and Common Figures

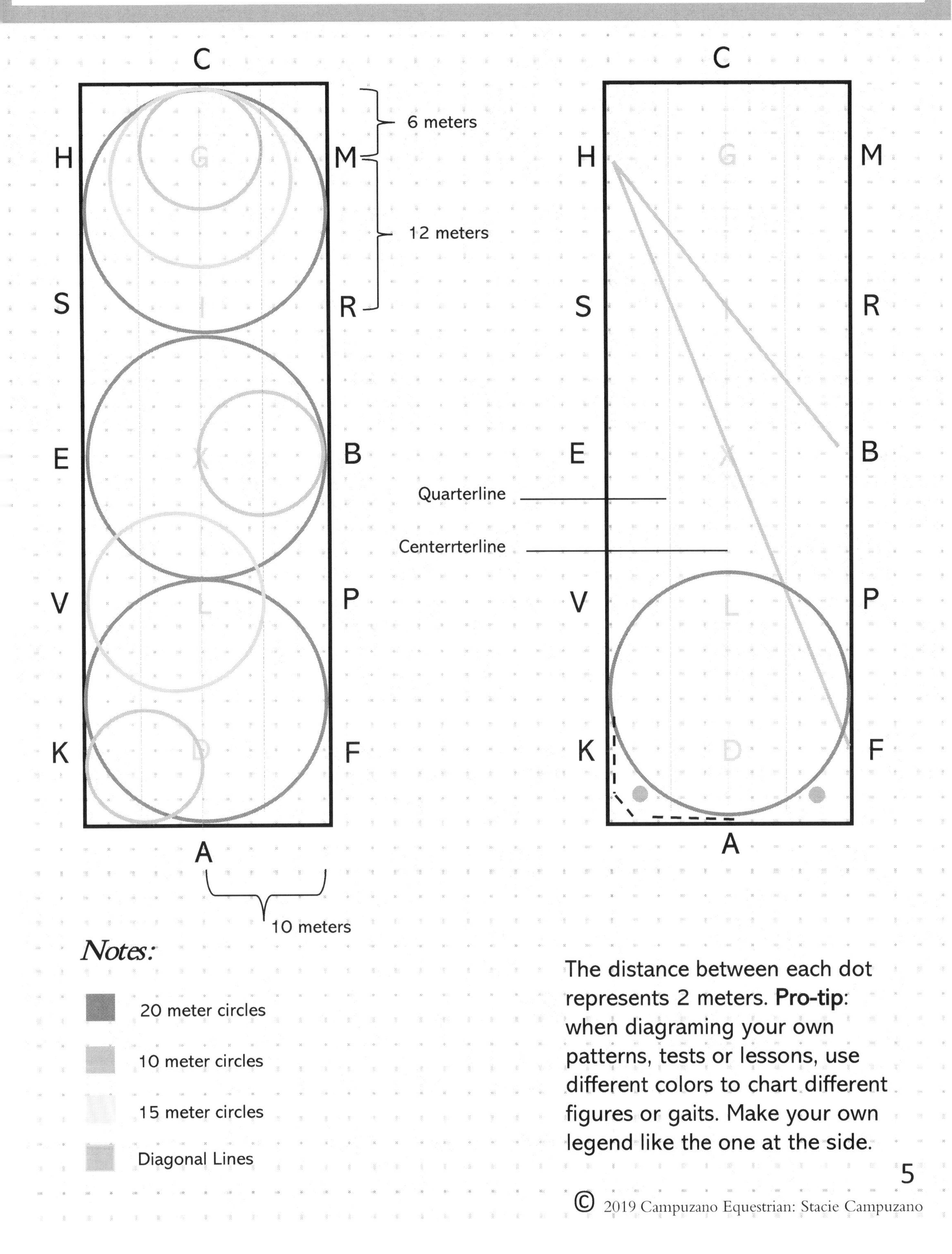

Notes:

20 meter circles

10 meter circles

15 meter circles

Diagonal Lines

The distance between each dot represents 2 meters. **Pro-tip**: when diagraming your own patterns, tests or lessons, use different colors to chart different figures or gaits. Make your own legend like the one at the side.

Instructor: Date:

Keywords/Visuals

Notes

Lesson Highlights

20 x 60 Meter Dressage Court

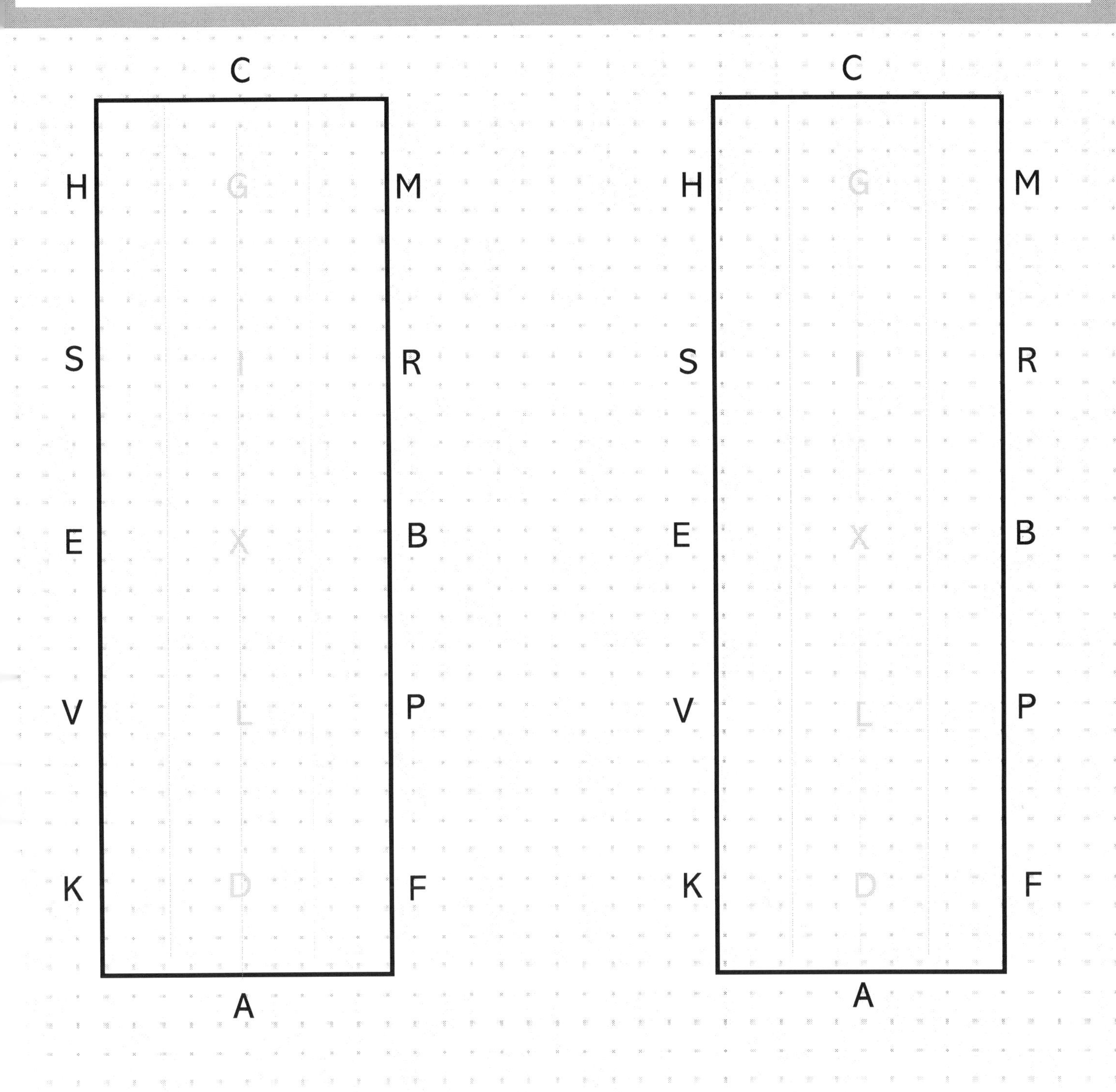

Notes:

Instructor: Date:

Keywords/Visuals	Notes

Lesson Highlights

20 x 60 Meter Dressage Court

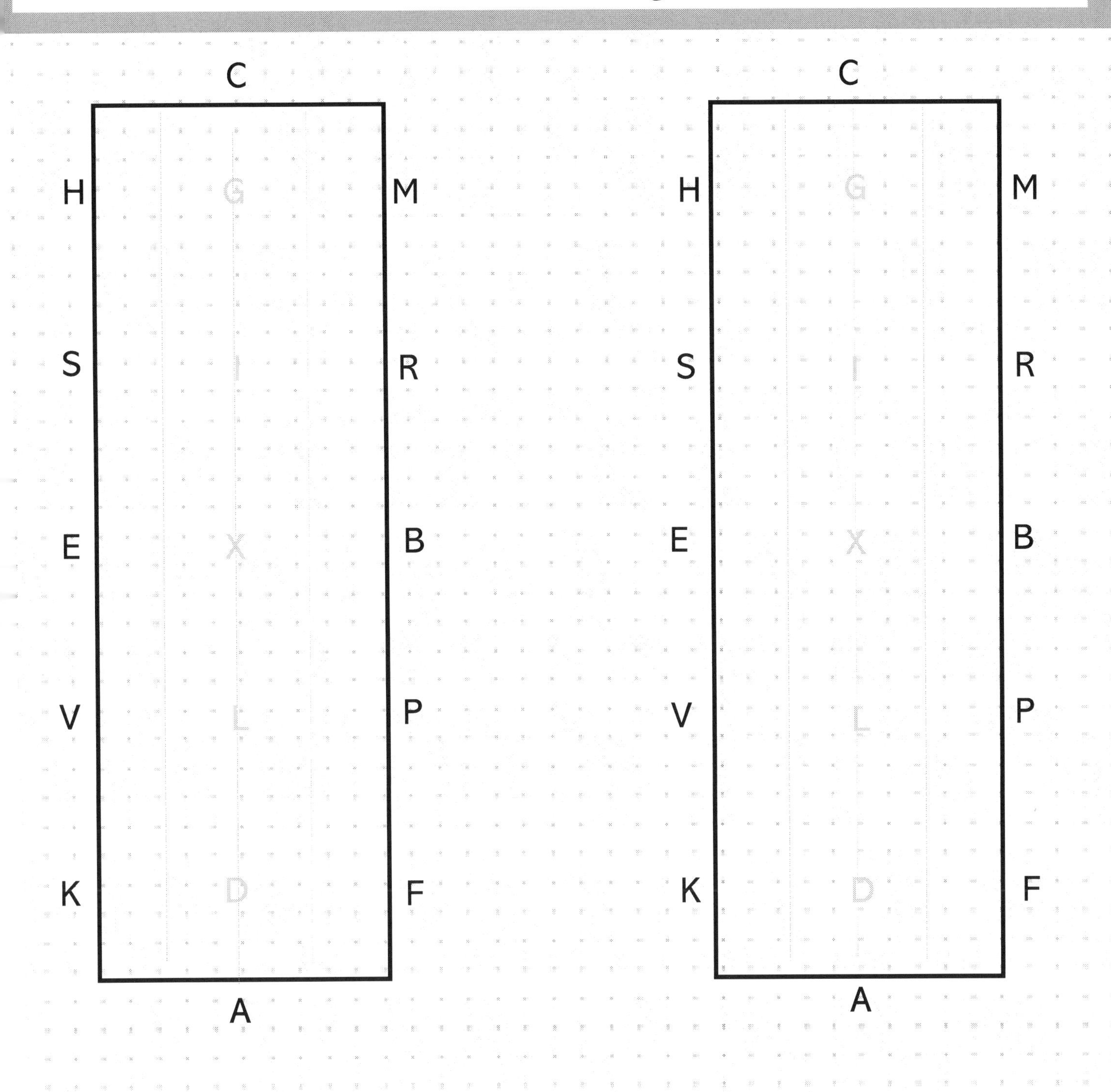

Notes:

Instructor: Date:

Keywords/Visuals	Notes

Lesson Highlights

20 x 60 Meter Dressage Court

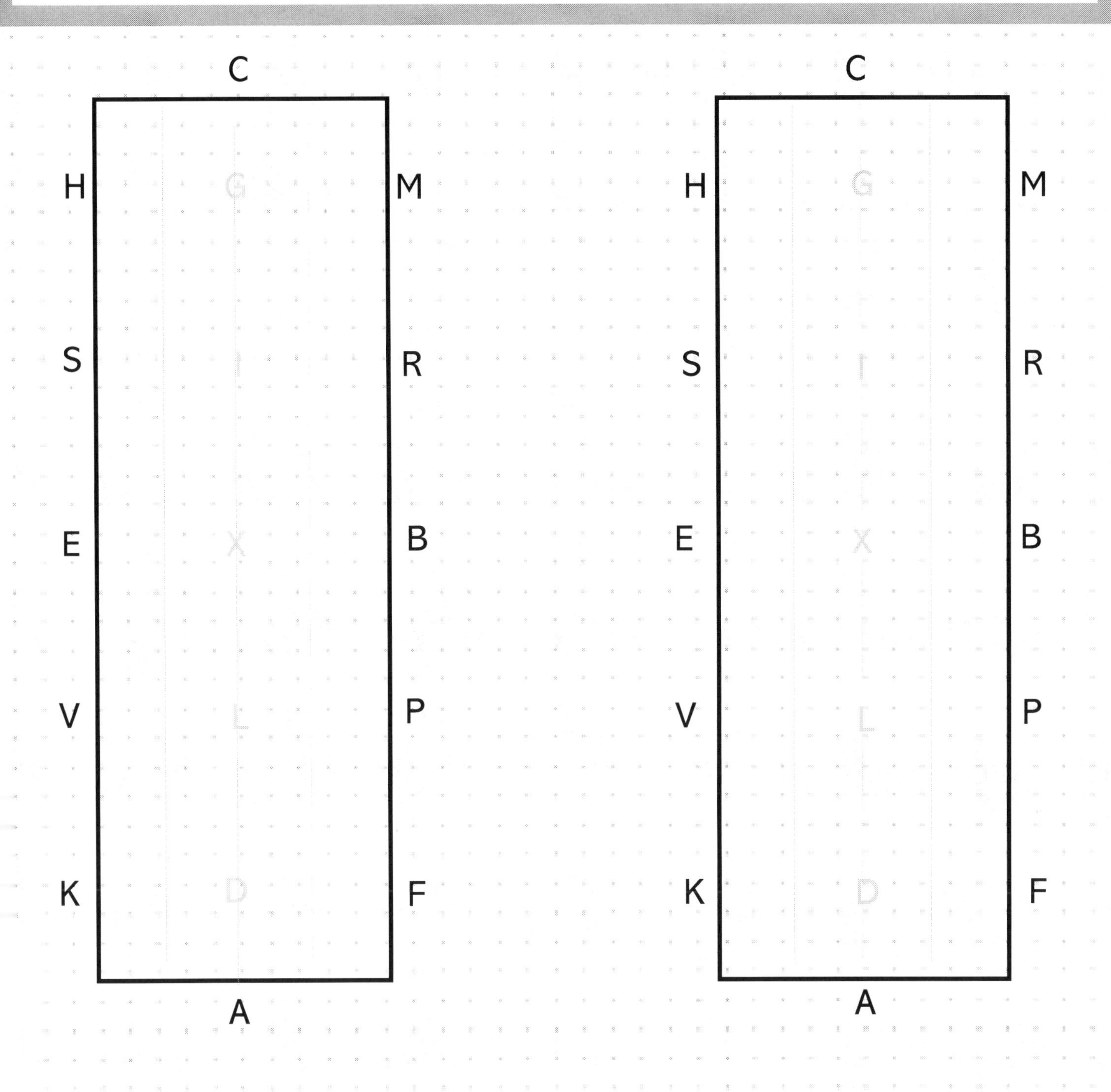

Notes:

Instructor: Date:

Keywords/Visuals	Notes

Lesson Highlights

20 x 60 Meter Dressage Court

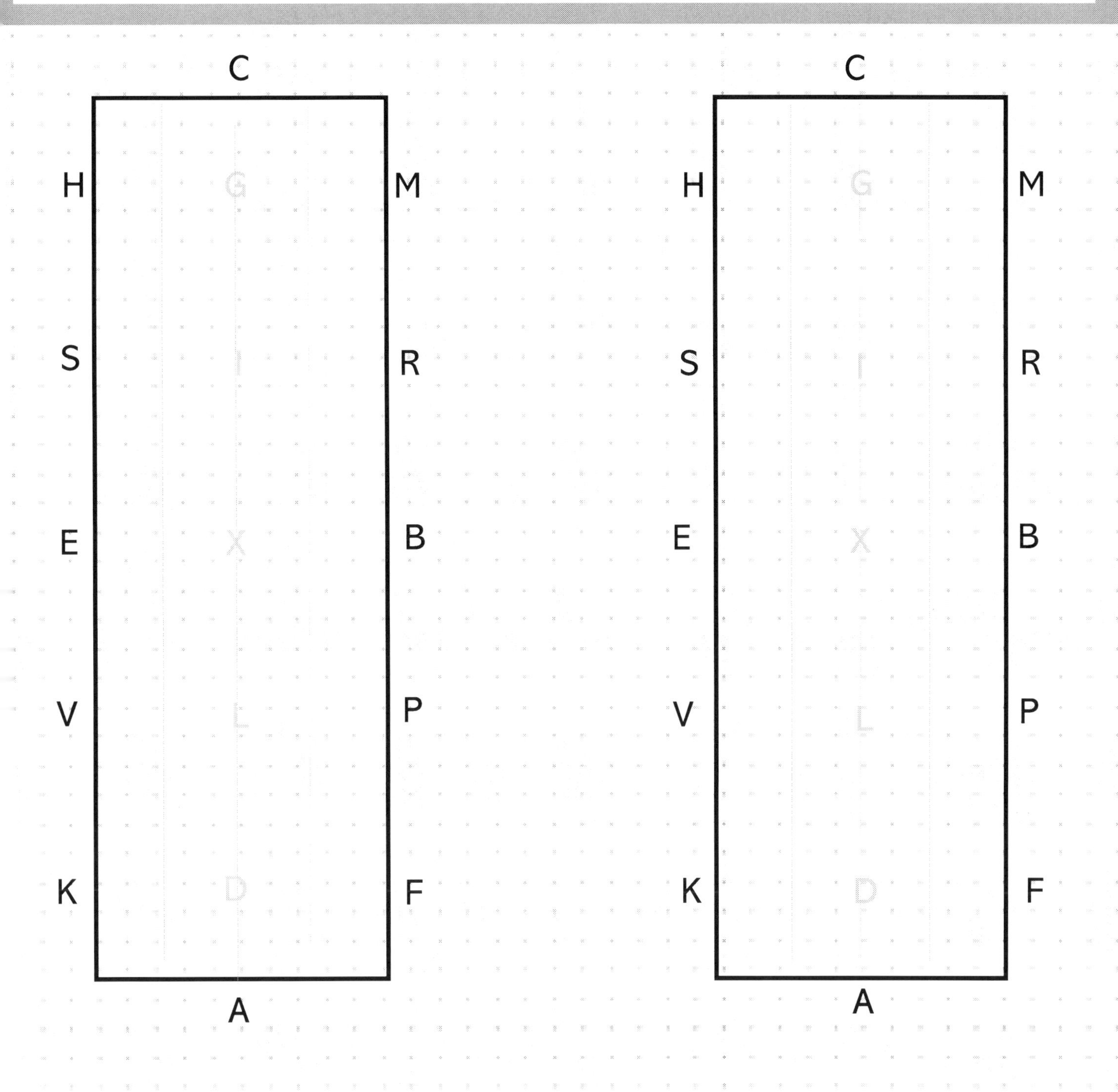

Notes:

Instructor: Date:

Keywords/Visuals	Notes

Lesson Highlights

20 x 60 Meter Dressage Court

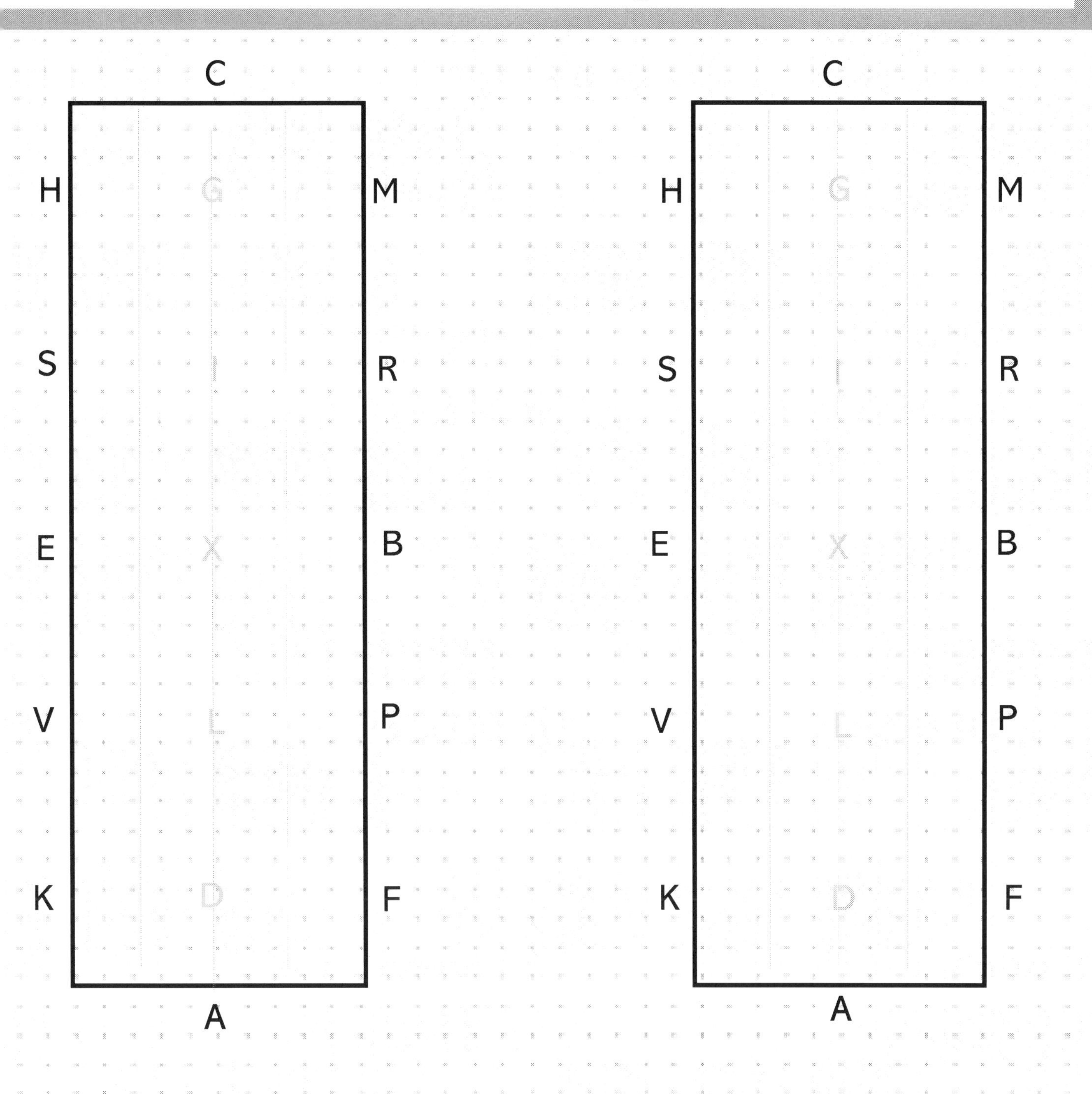

Notes:

Instructor: Date:

Keywords/Visuals

Notes

Lesson Highlights

20 x 60 Meter Dressage Court

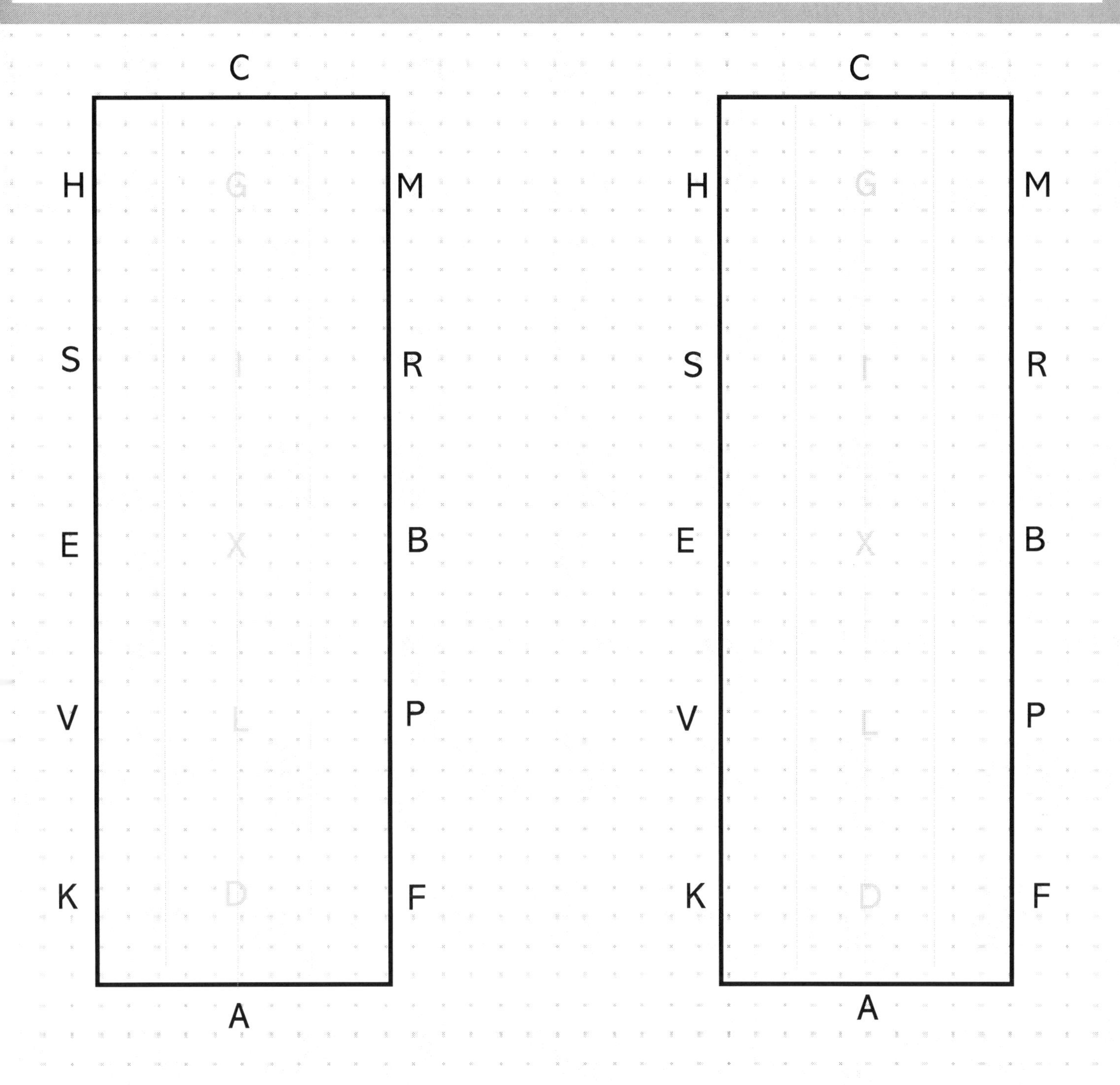

Notes:

Instructor: Date:

Keywords/Visuals

Notes

Lesson Highlights

20 x 60 Meter Dressage Court

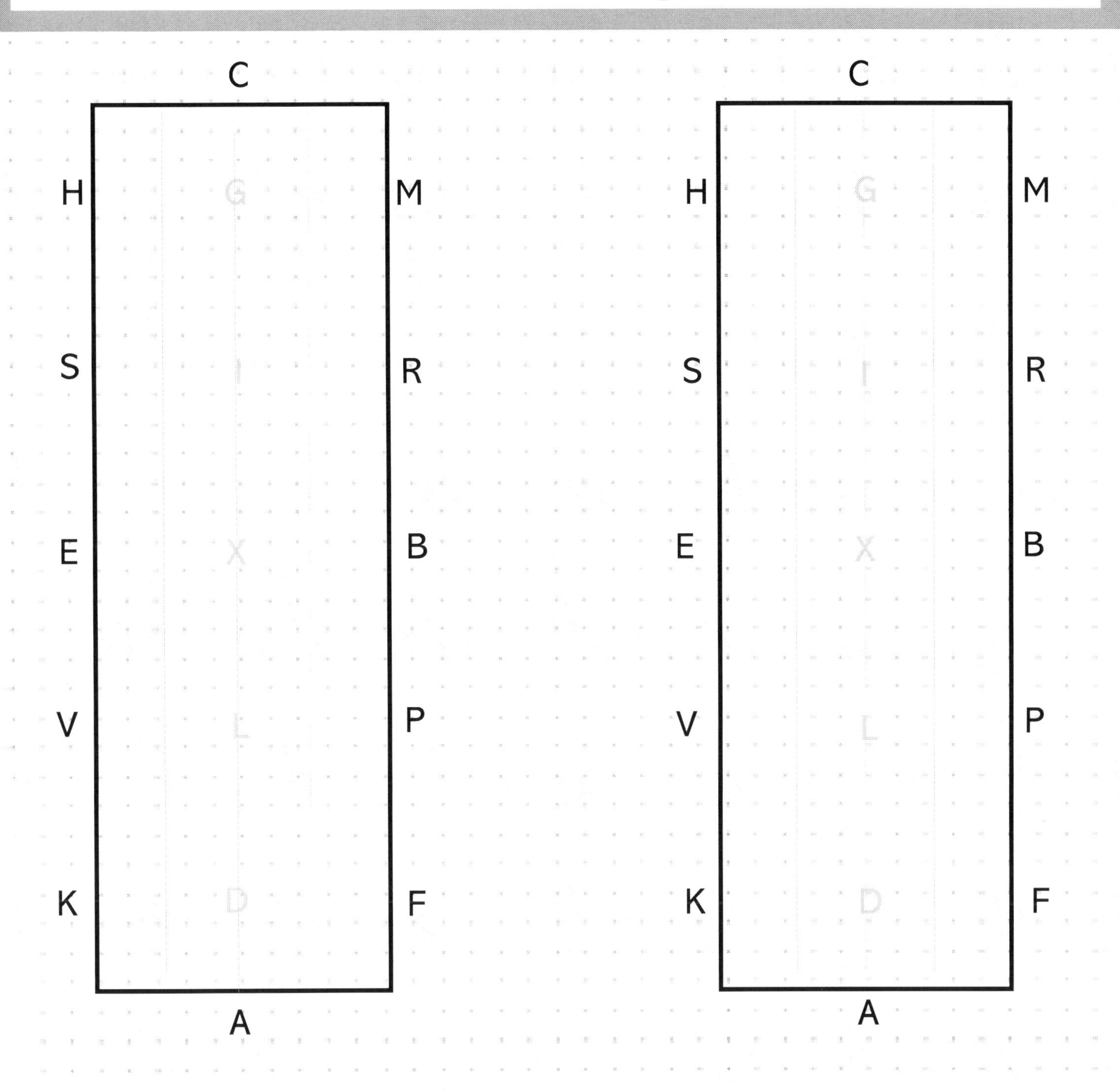

Notes:

Instructor: Date:

Keywords/Visuals

Notes

Lesson Highlights

20 x 60 Meter Dressage Court

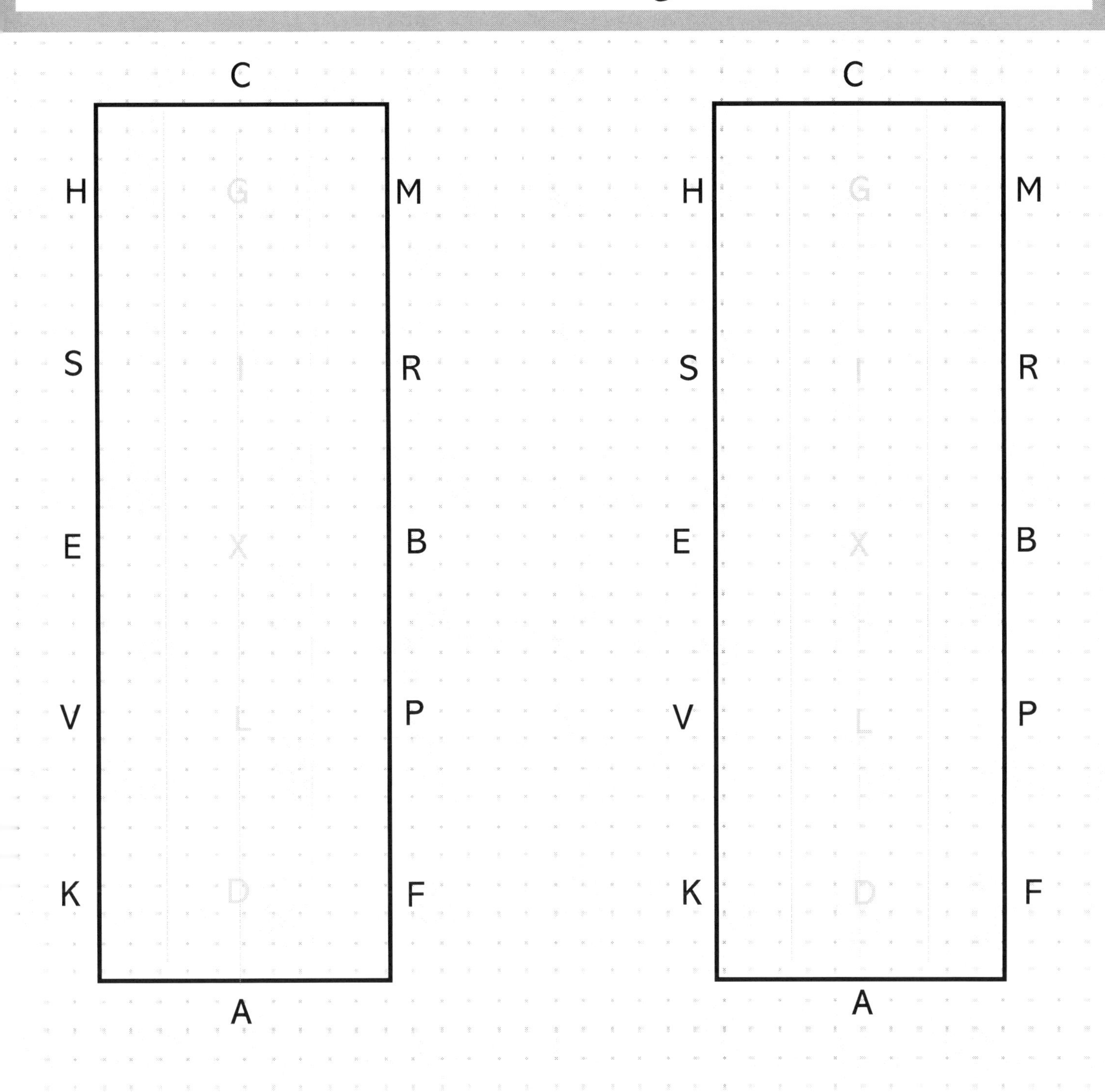

Notes:

Instructor: Date:

Keywords/Visuals

Notes

Lesson Highlights

20 x 60 Meter Dressage Court

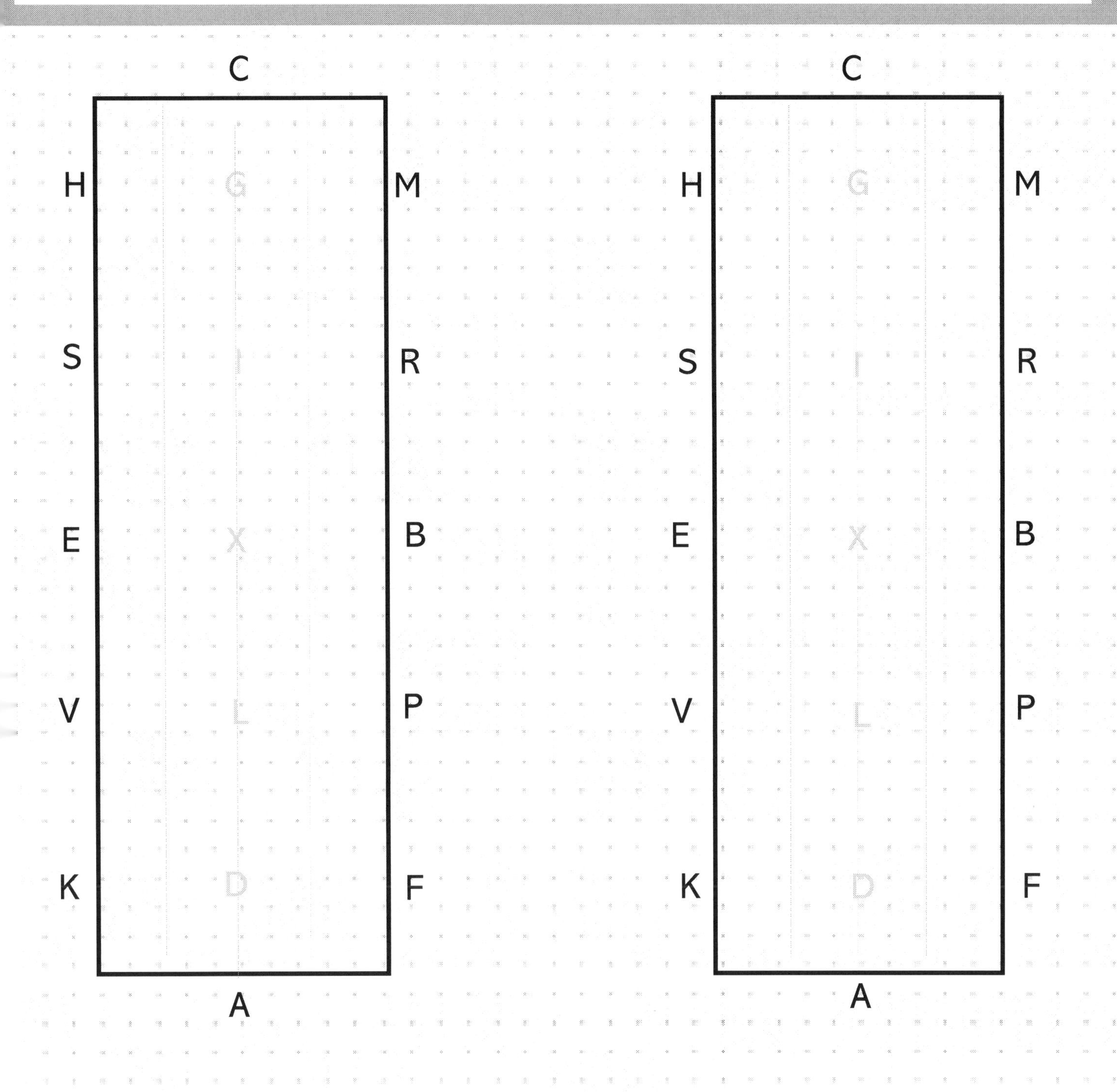

Notes:

Instructor: Date:

Keywords/Visuals

Notes

Lesson Highlights

20 x 60 Meter Dressage Court

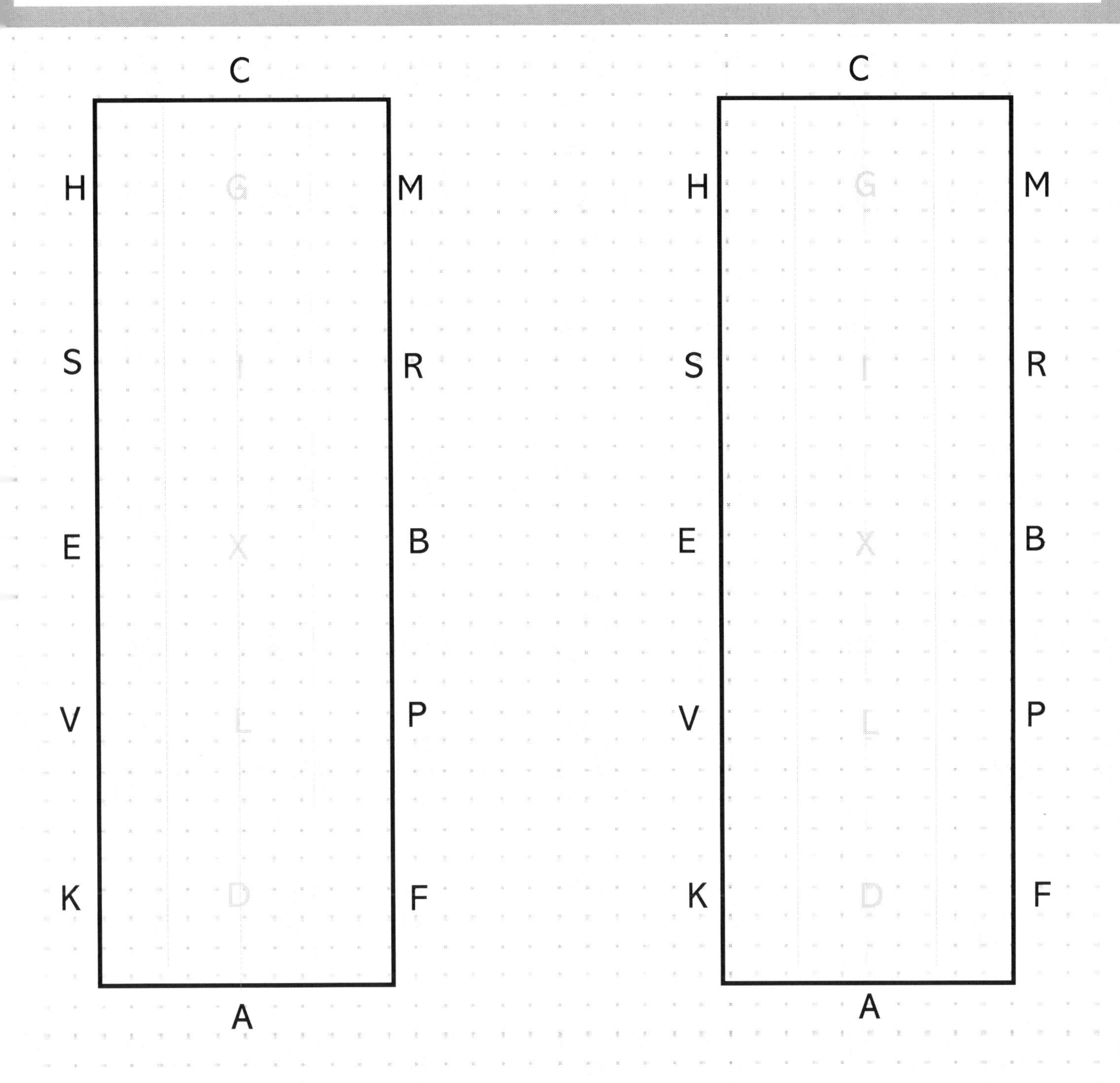

Notes:

Instructor: Date:

Keywords/Visuals

Notes

Lesson Highlights

20 x 60 Meter Dressage Court

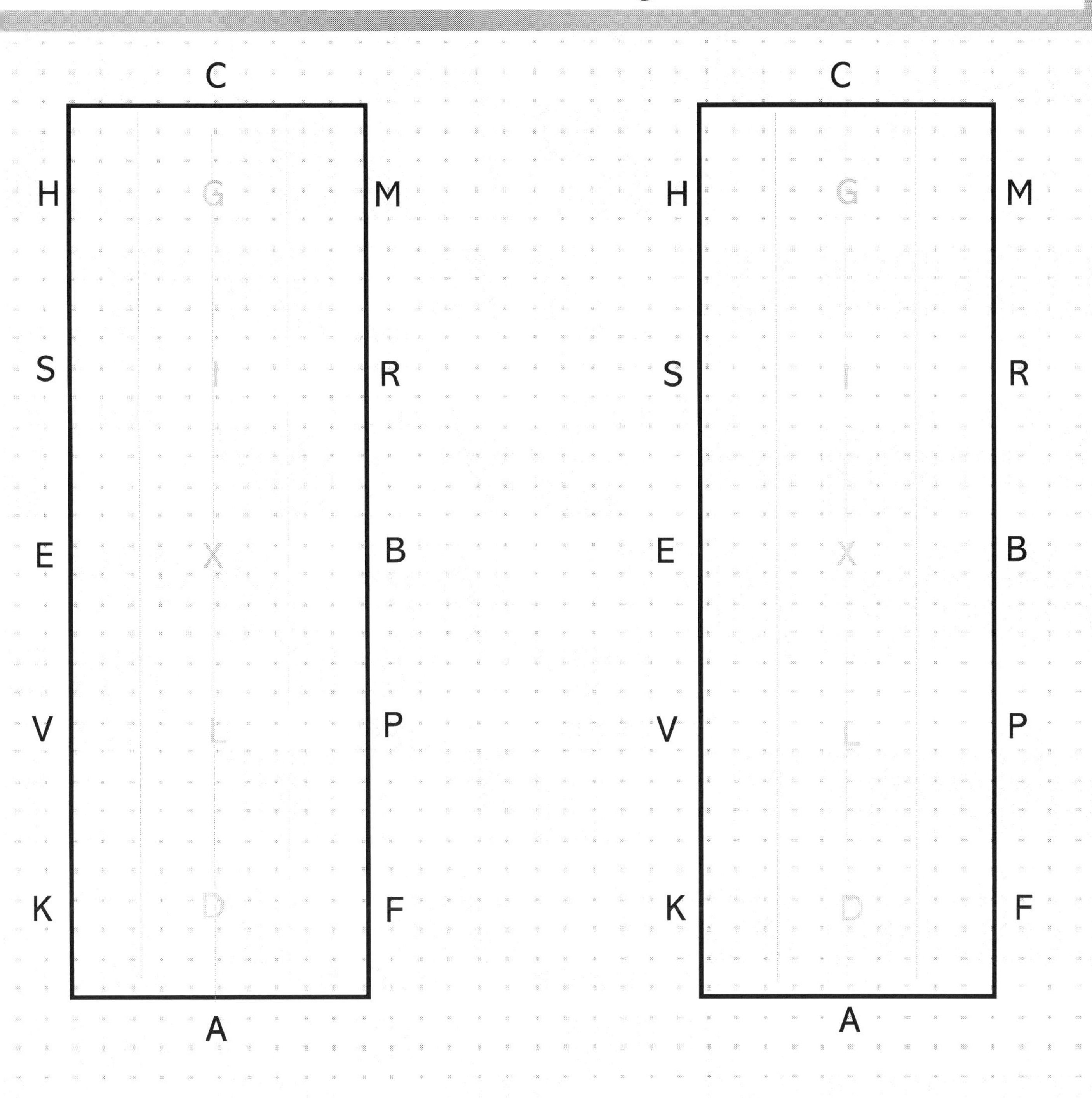

Notes:

Instructor: Date:

Keywords/Visuals

Notes

Lesson Highlights

20 x 60 Meter Dressage Court

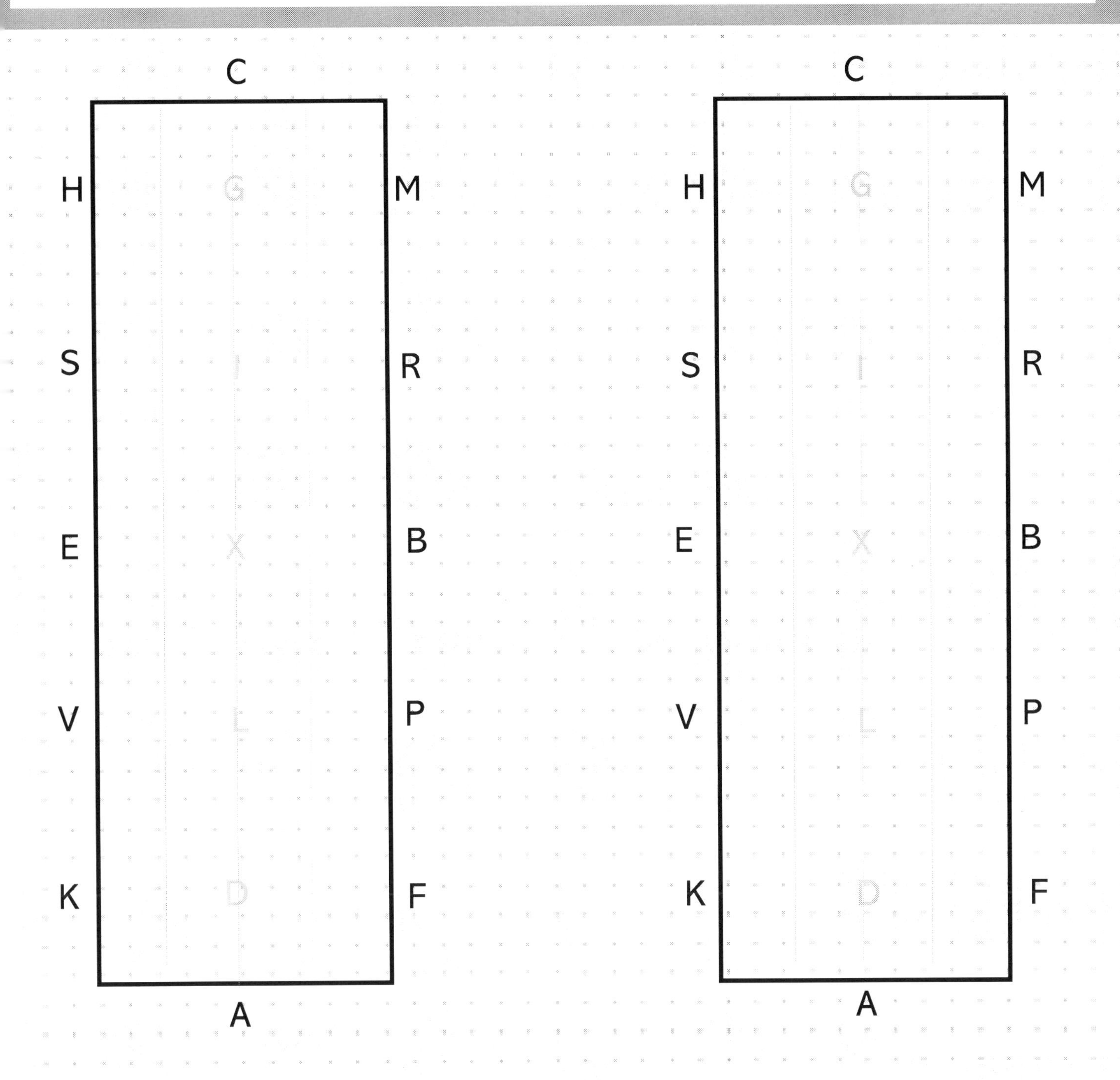

Notes:

Instructor: Date:

Keywords/Visuals

Notes

Lesson Highlights

20 x 60 Meter Dressage Court

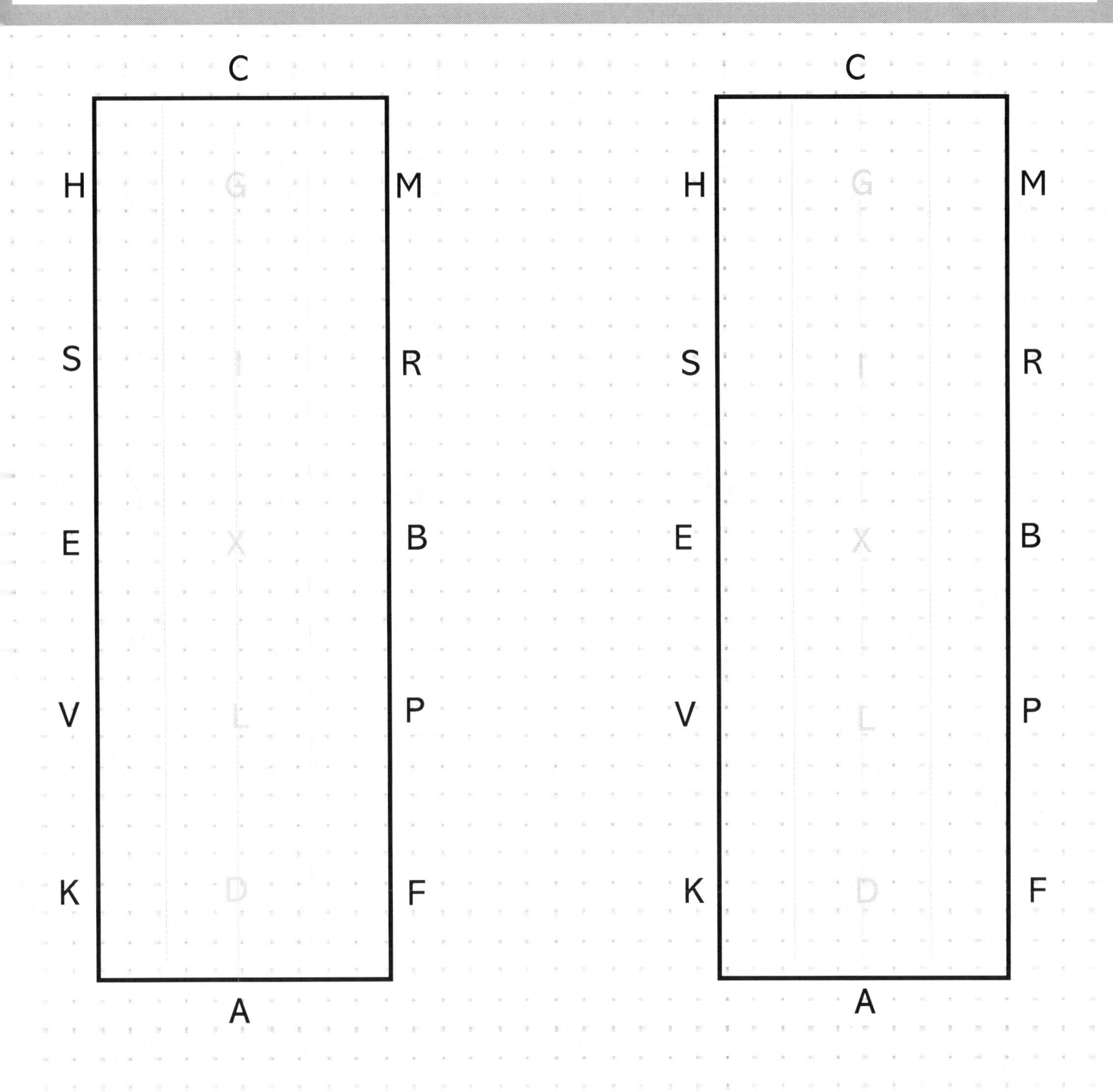

Notes:

Instructor: Date:

Keywords/Visuals

Notes

Lesson Highlights

20 x 60 Meter Dressage Court

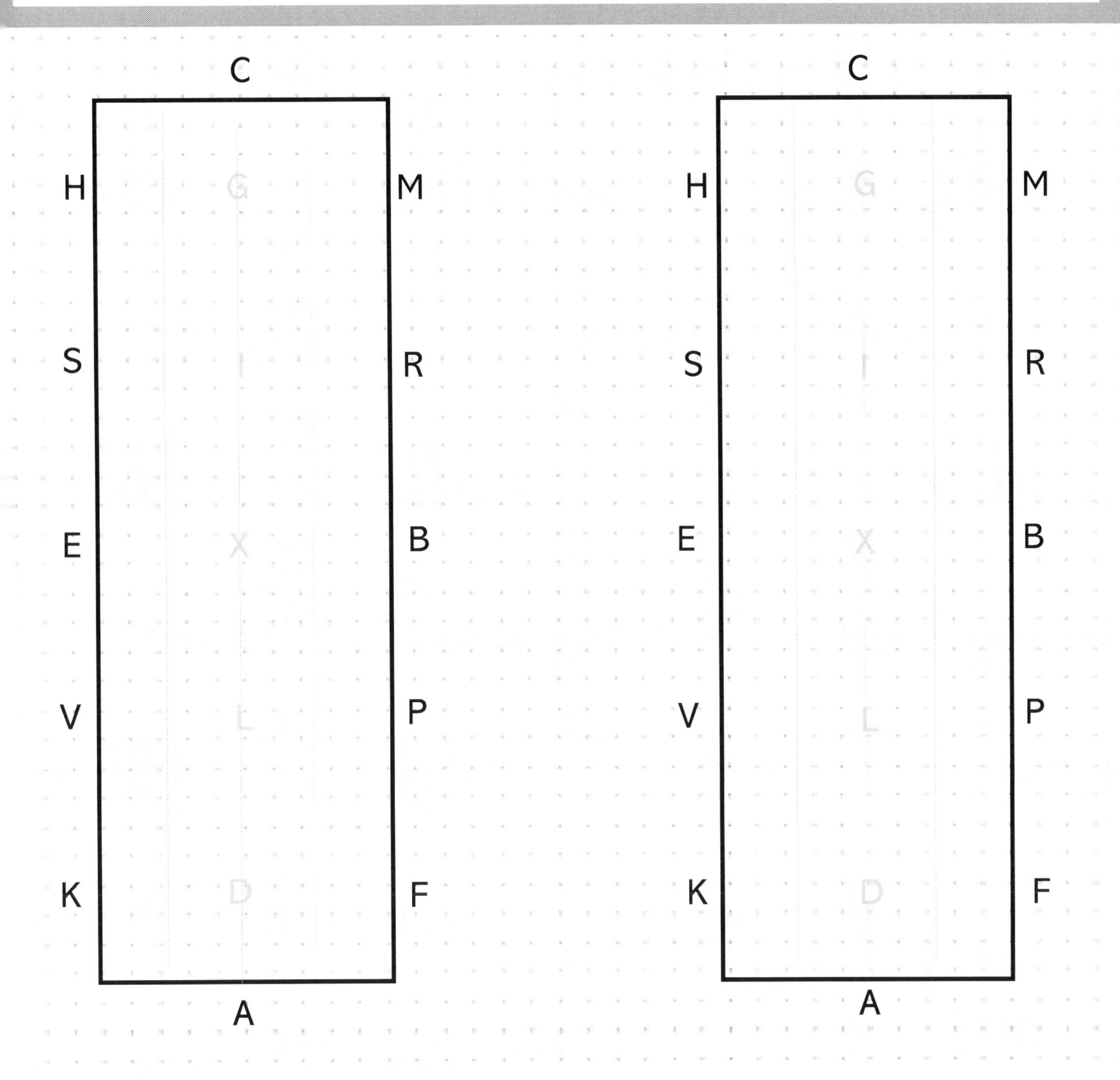

Notes:

Instructor: Date:

Keywords/Visuals

Notes

Lesson Highlights

20 x 60 Meter Dressage Court

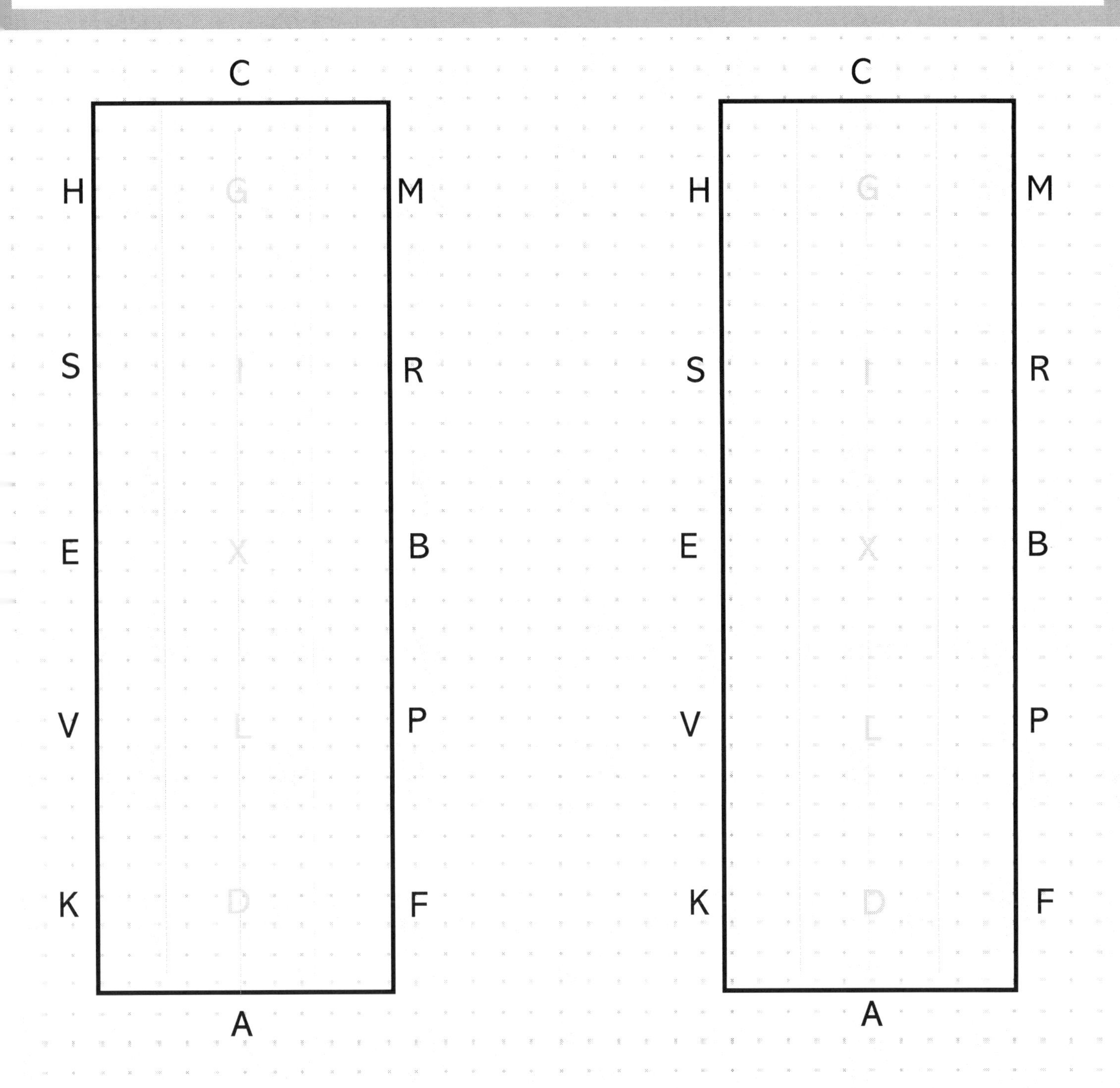

Notes:

Instructor: Date:

Keywords/Visuals

Notes

Lesson Highlights

20 x 60 Meter Dressage Court

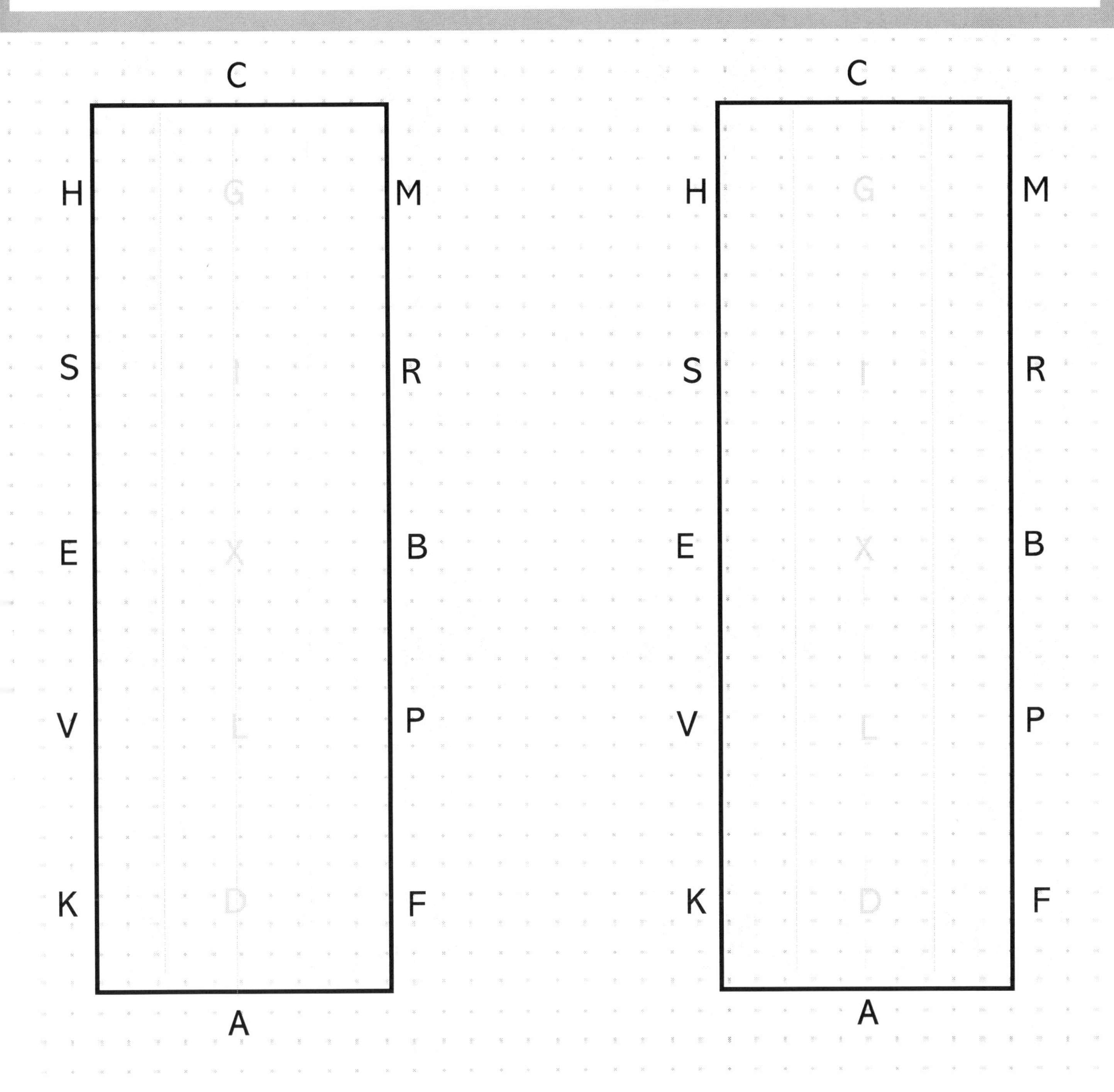

Notes:

Instructor: Date:

Keywords/Visuals	Notes

Lesson Highlights

20 x 60 Meter Dressage Court

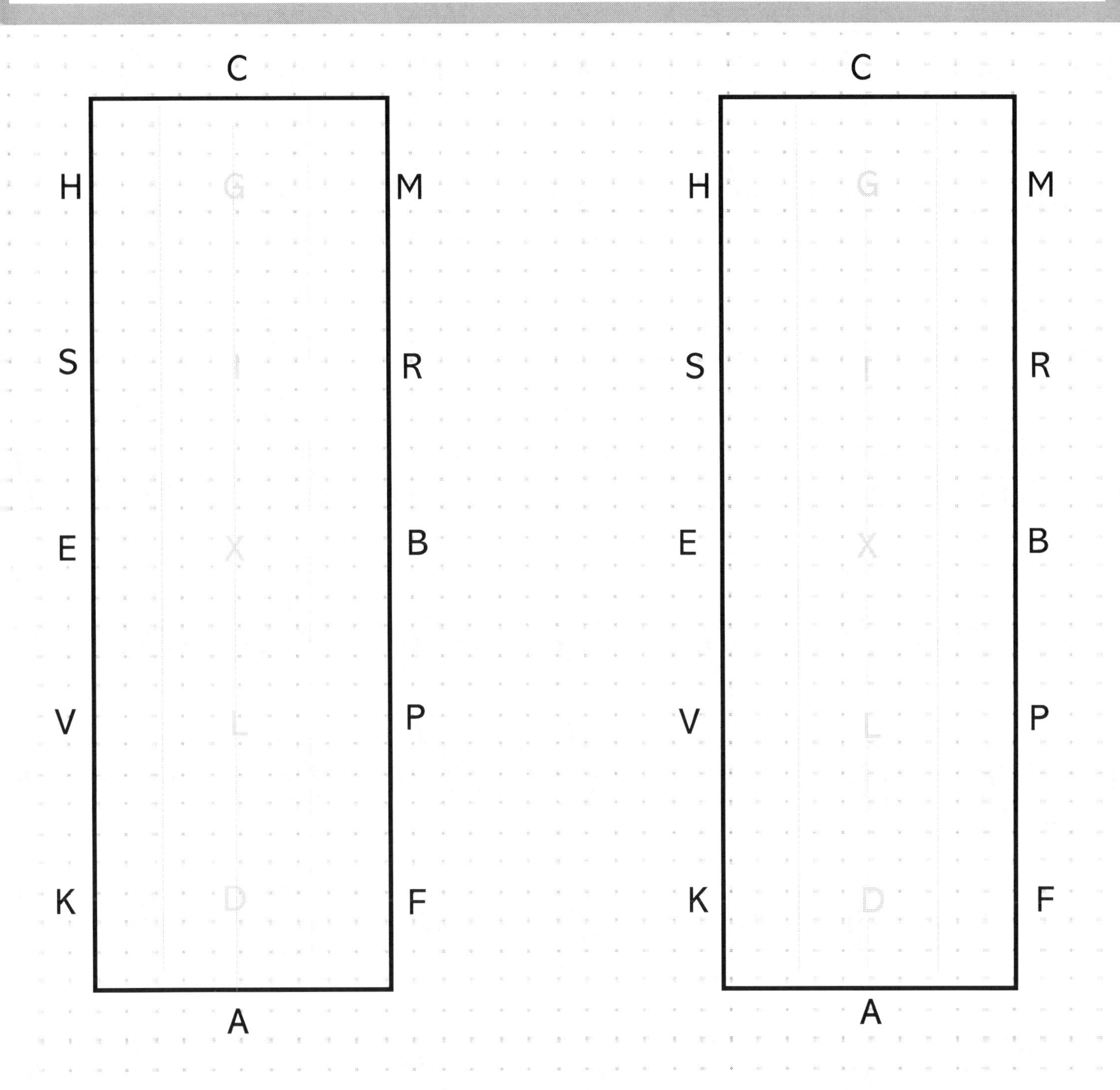

Notes:

Instructor: Date:

Keywords/Visuals

Notes

Lesson Highlights

20 x 60 Meter Dressage Court

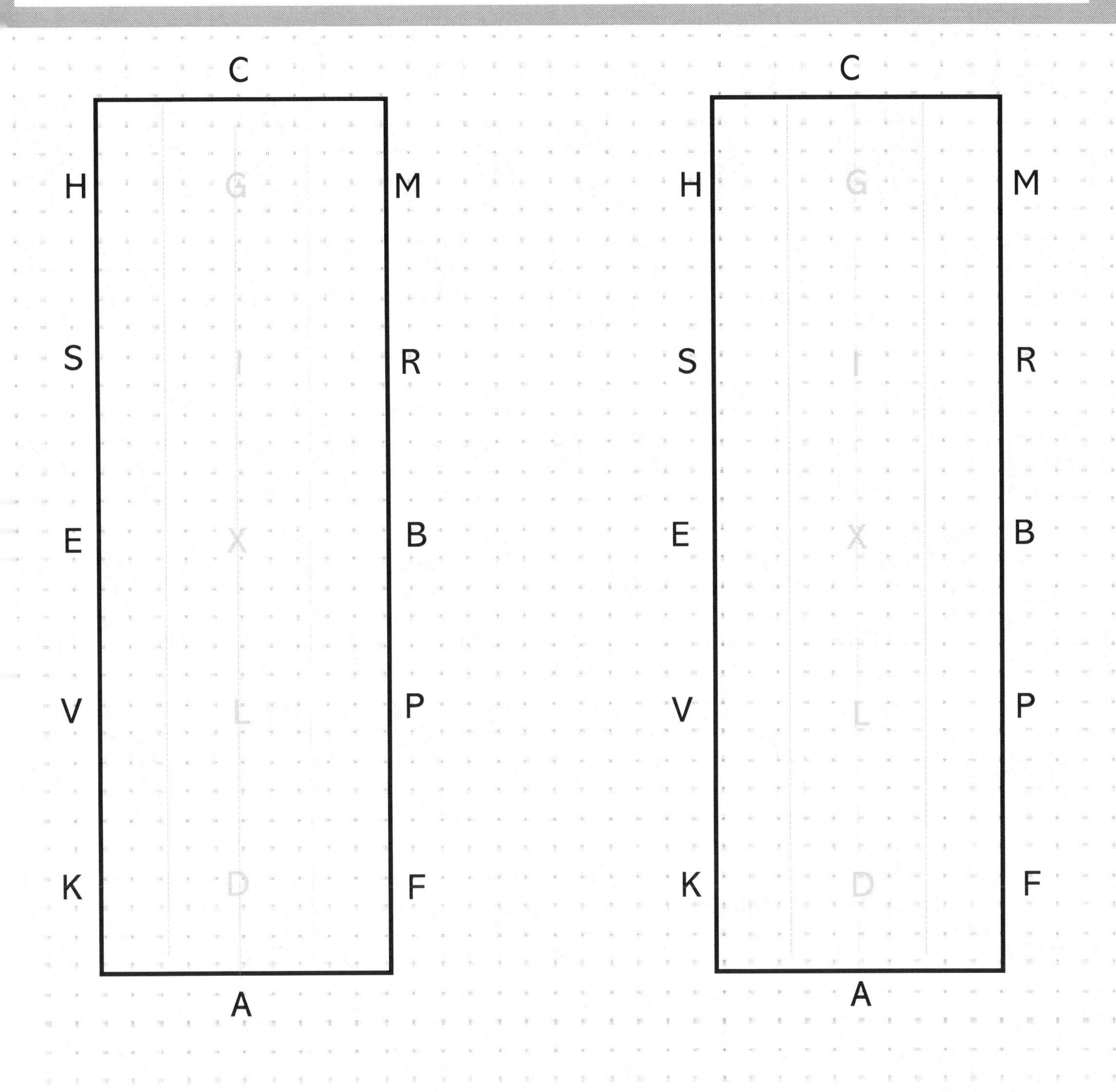

Notes:

Instructor: Date:

Keywords/Visuals	Notes

Lesson Highlights

20 x 60 Meter Dressage Court

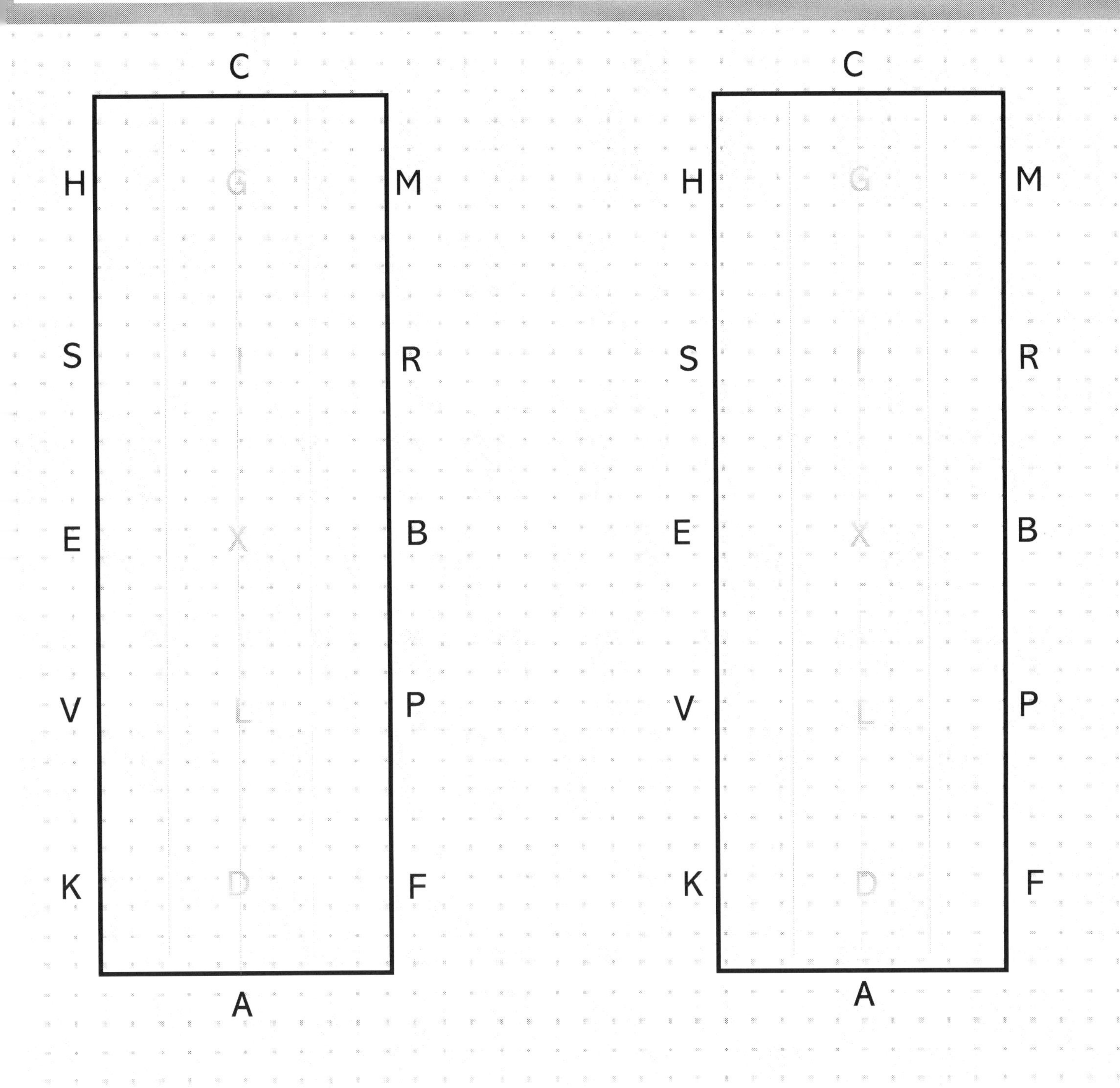

Notes:

Instructor: Date:

Keywords/Visuals

Notes

Lesson Highlights

20 x 60 Meter Dressage Court

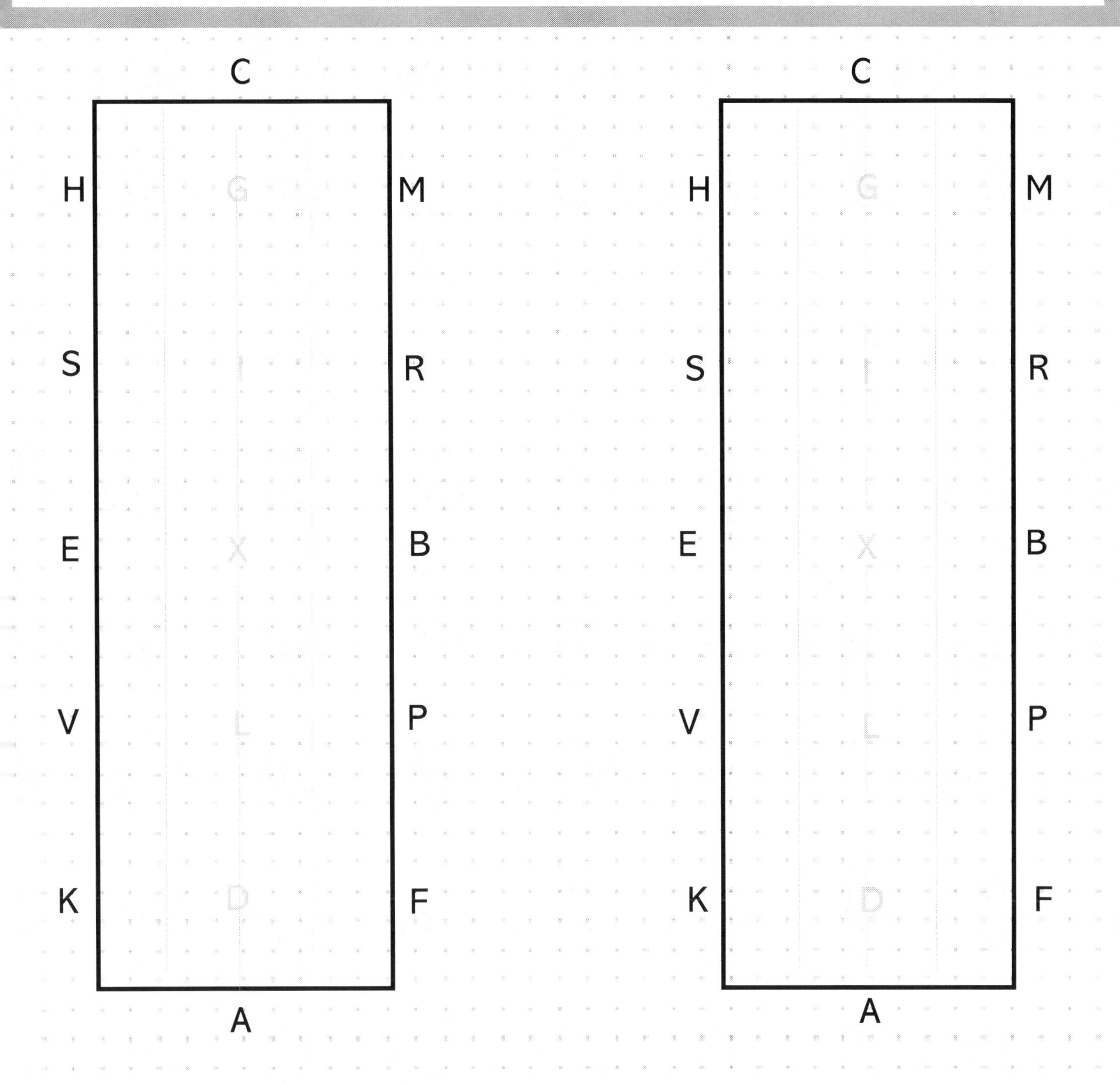

Notes:

Instructor: Date:

Keywords/Visuals	Notes

Lesson Highlights

20 x 60 Meter Dressage Court

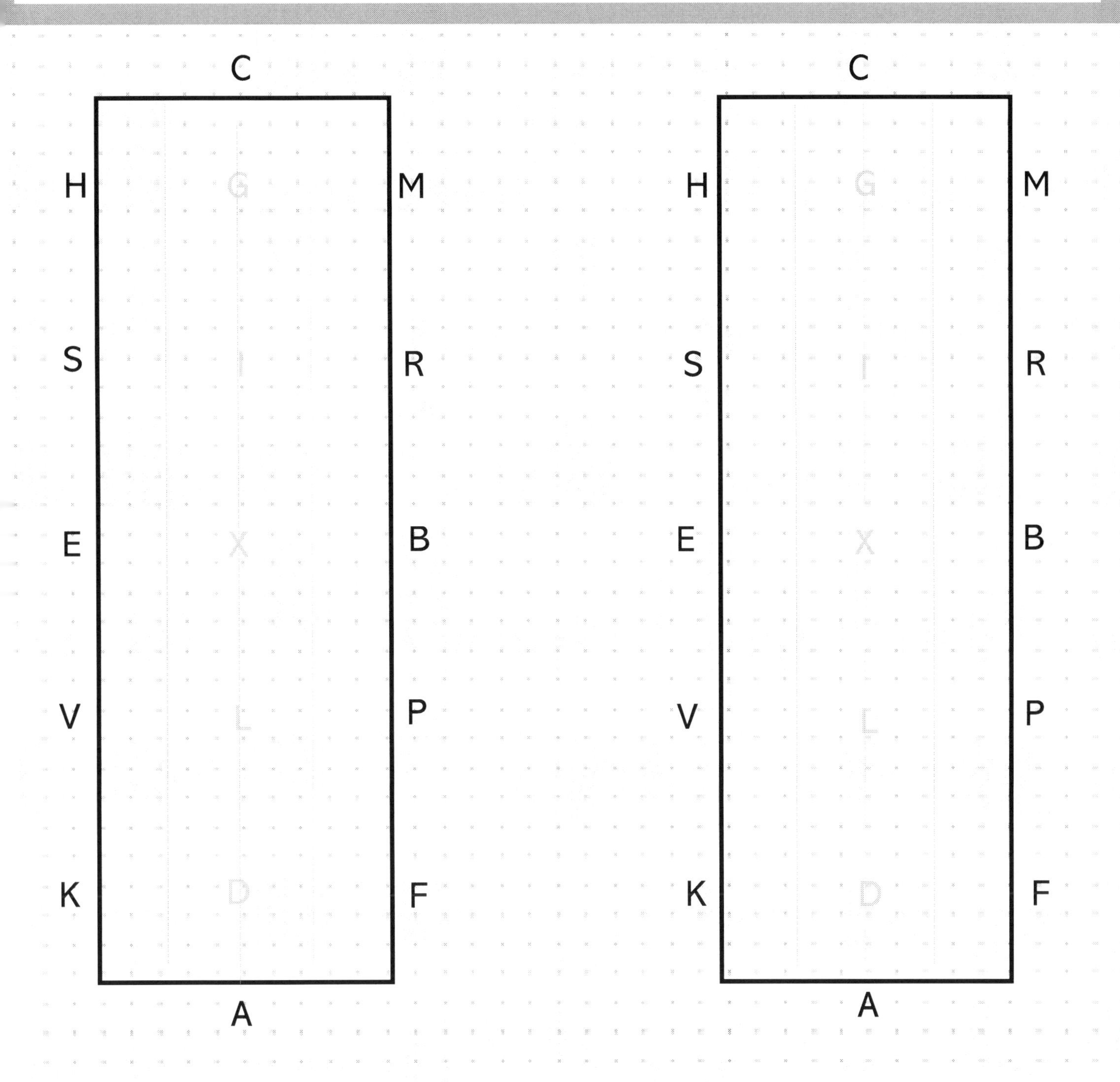

Notes:

Instructor: Date:

Keywords/Visuals	Notes

Lesson Highlights

20 x 60 Meter Dressage Court

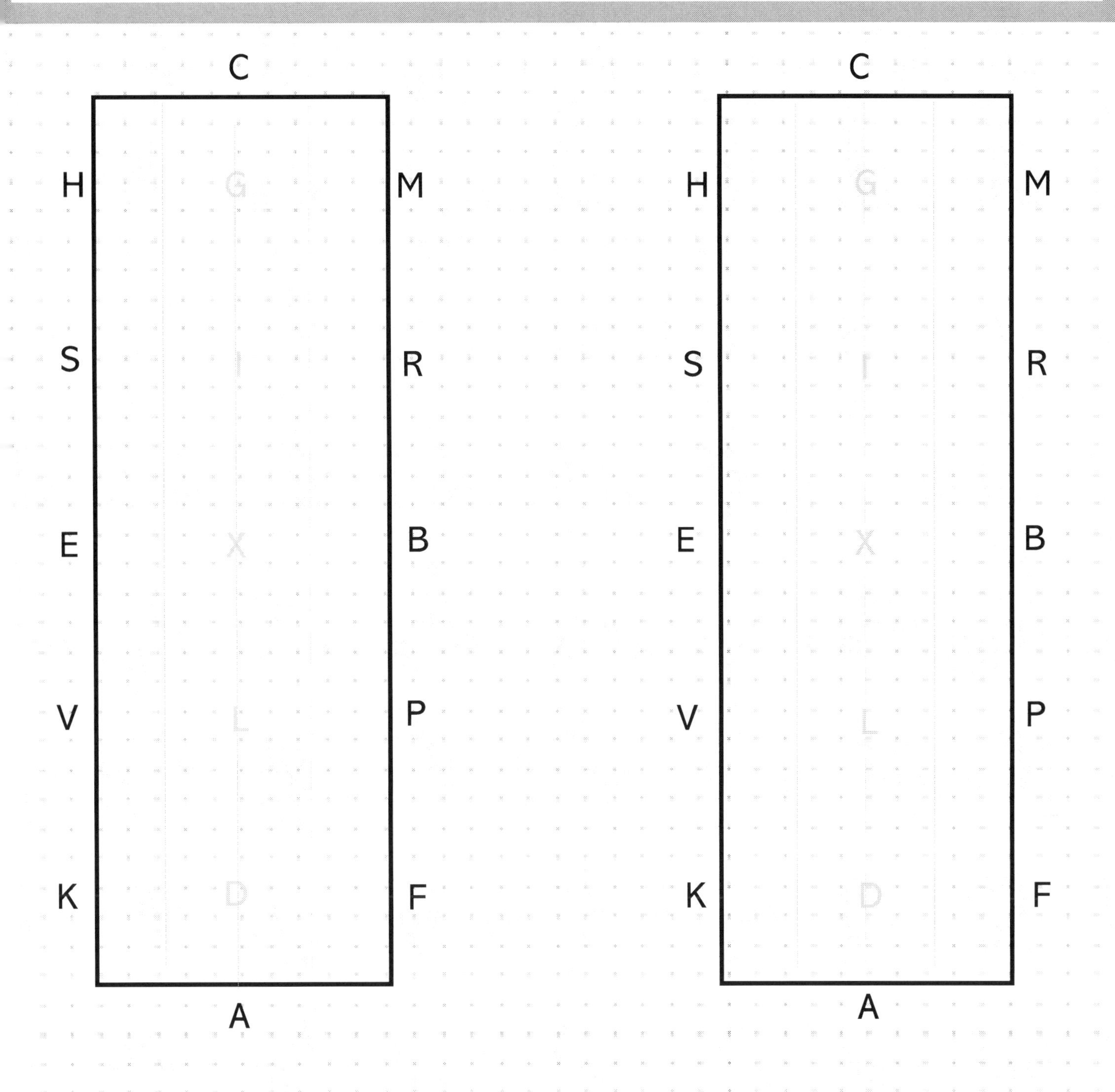

Notes:

Instructor: Date:

Keywords/Visuals

Notes

Lesson Highlights

20 x 60 Meter Dressage Court

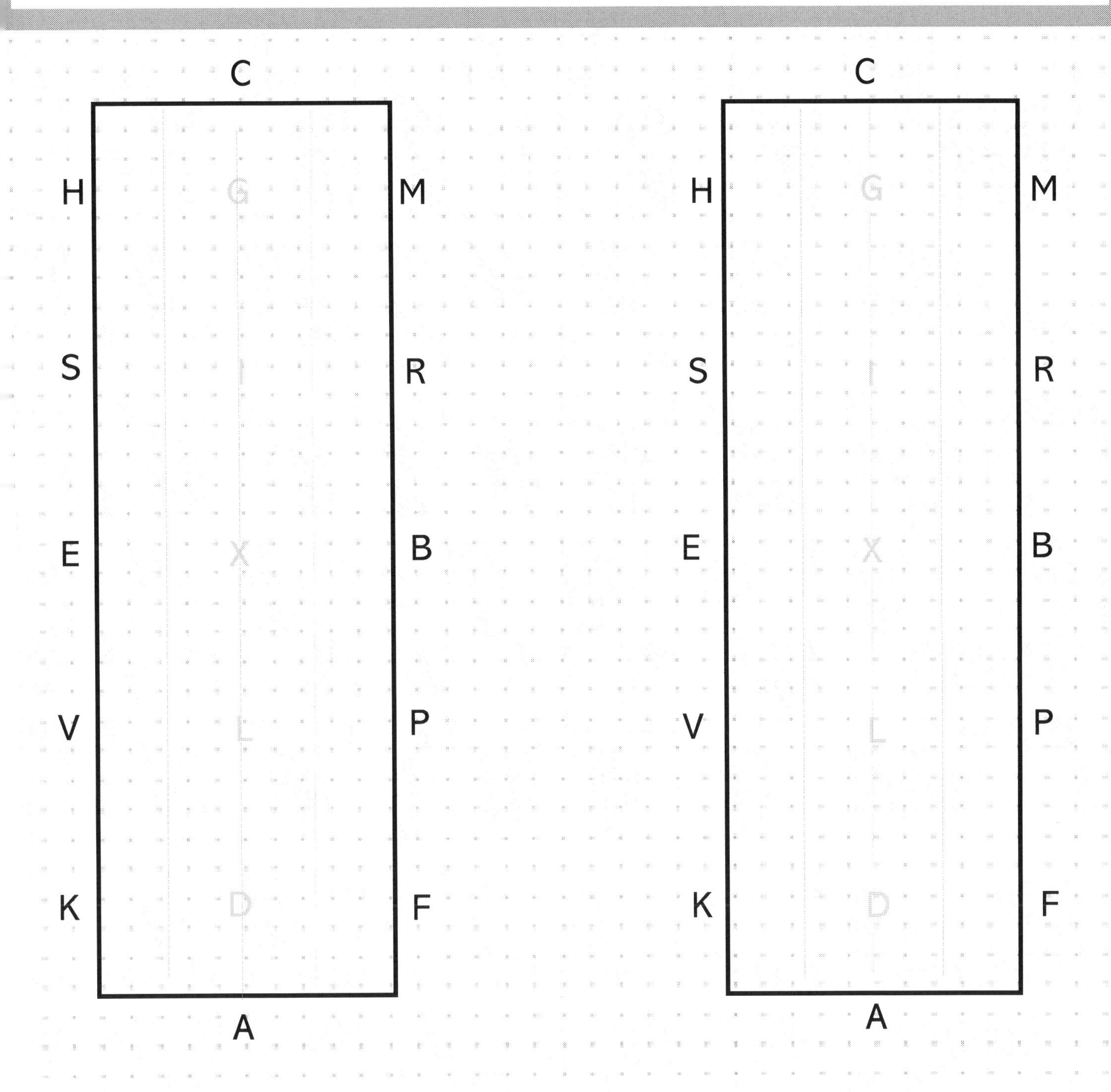

Notes:

Instructor: Date:

Keywords/Visuals

Notes

Lesson Highlights

20 x 60 Meter Dressage Court

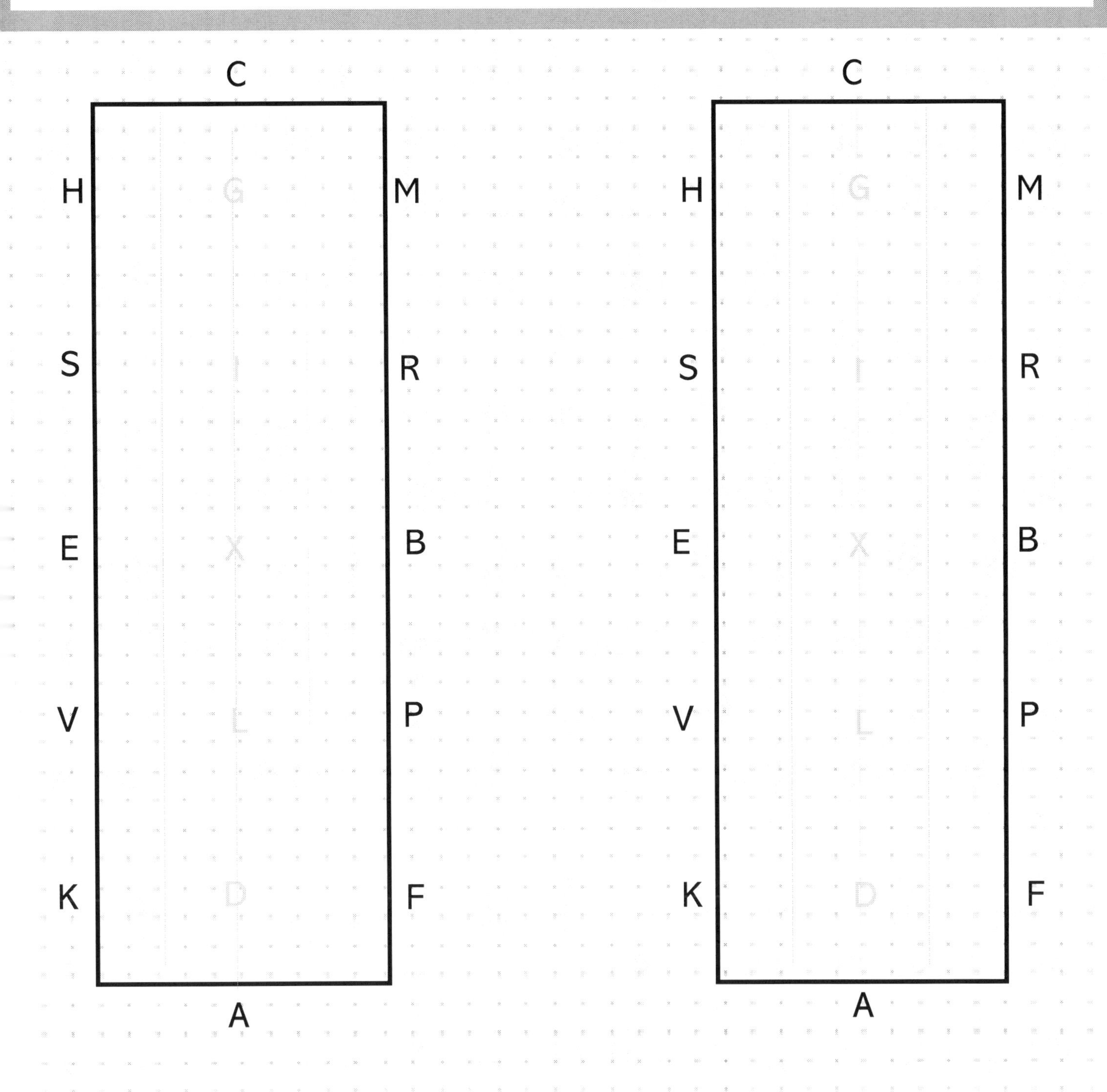

Notes:

Instructor: Date:

Keywords/Visuals	Notes

Lesson Highlights

20 x 60 Meter Dressage Court

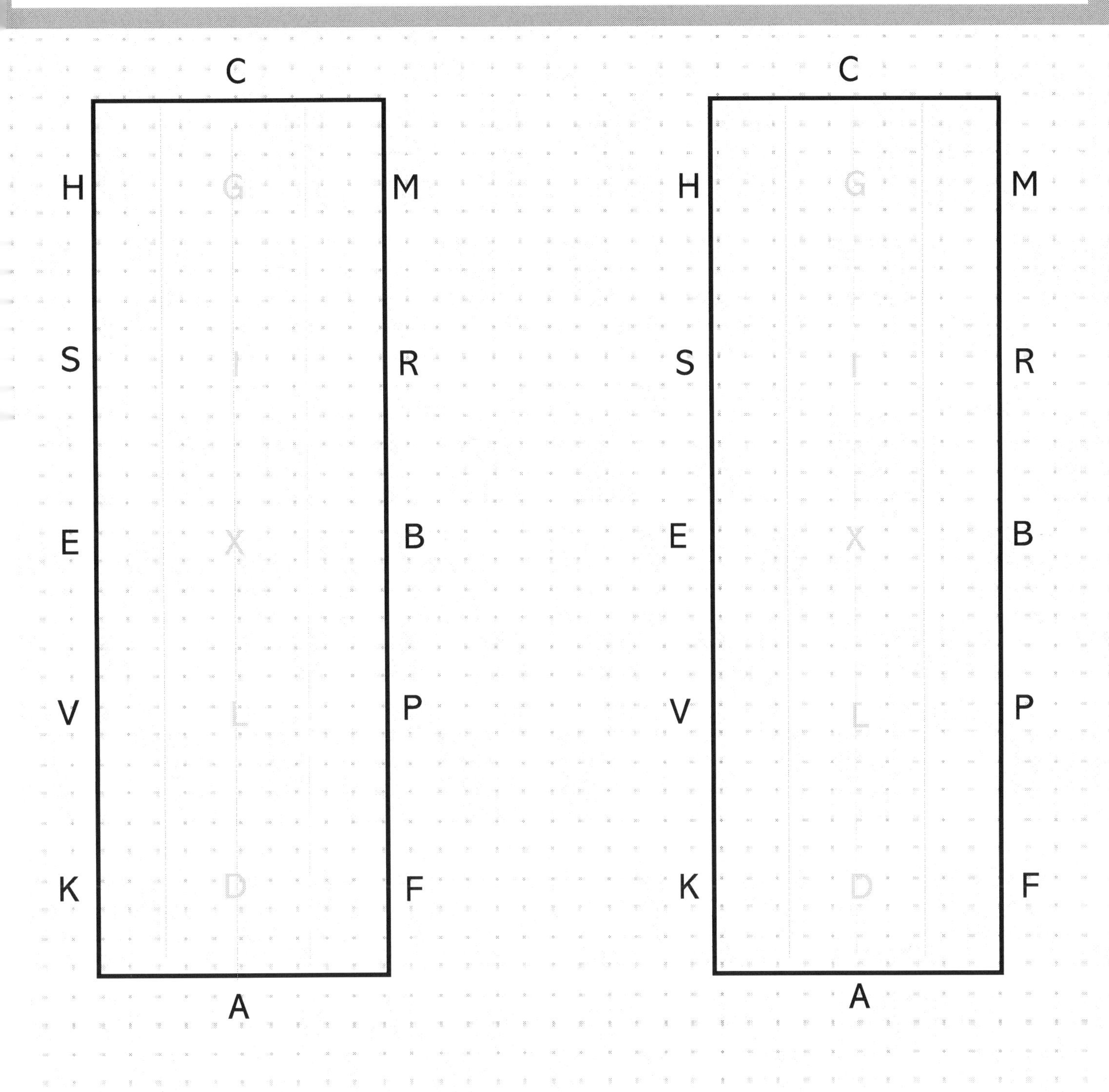

Notes:

Instructor: Date:

Keywords/Visuals

Notes

Lesson Highlights

20 x 60 Meter Dressage Court

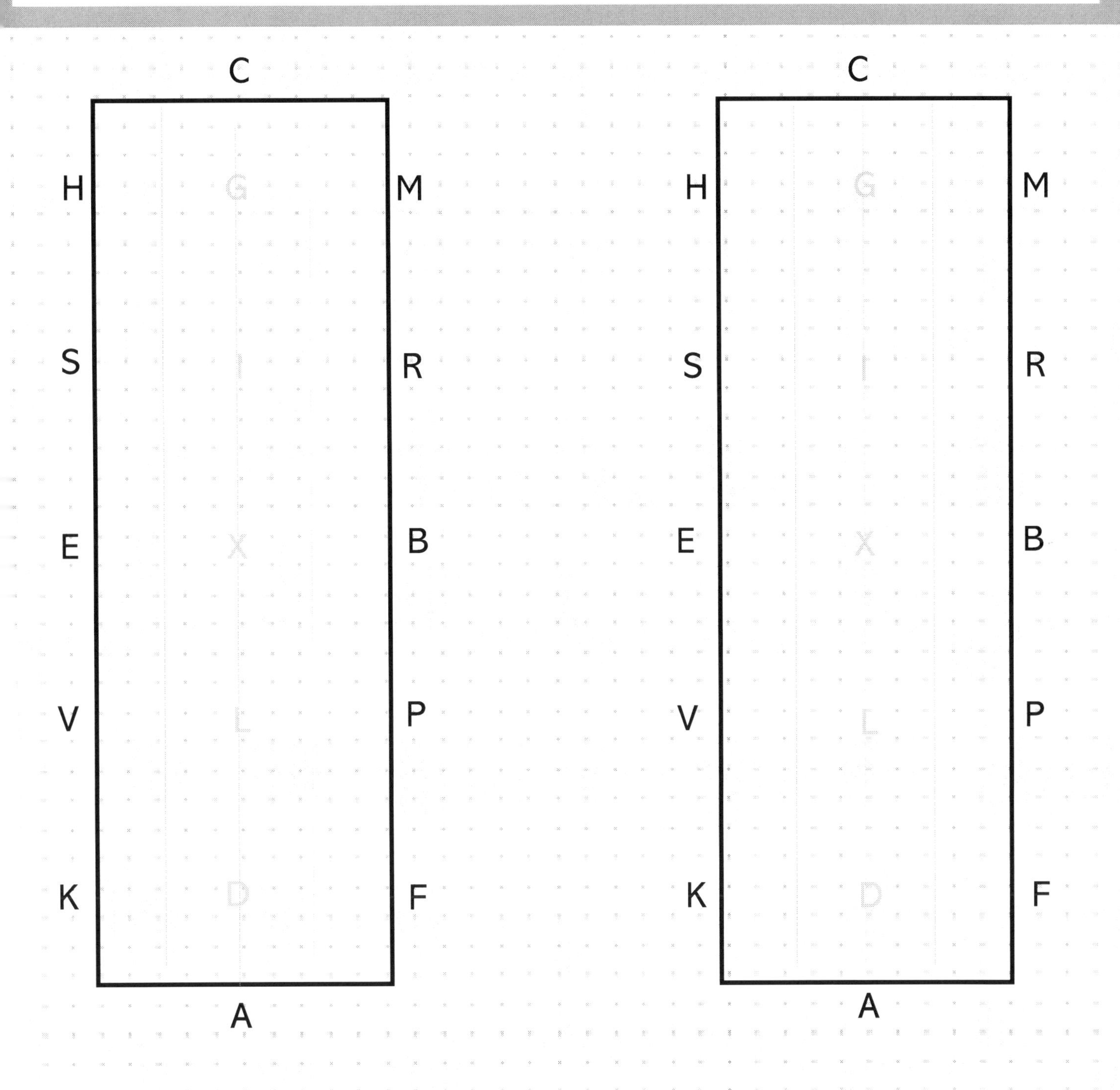

Notes:

Instructor: Date:

Keywords/Visuals

Notes

Lesson Highlights

20 x 60 Meter Dressage Court

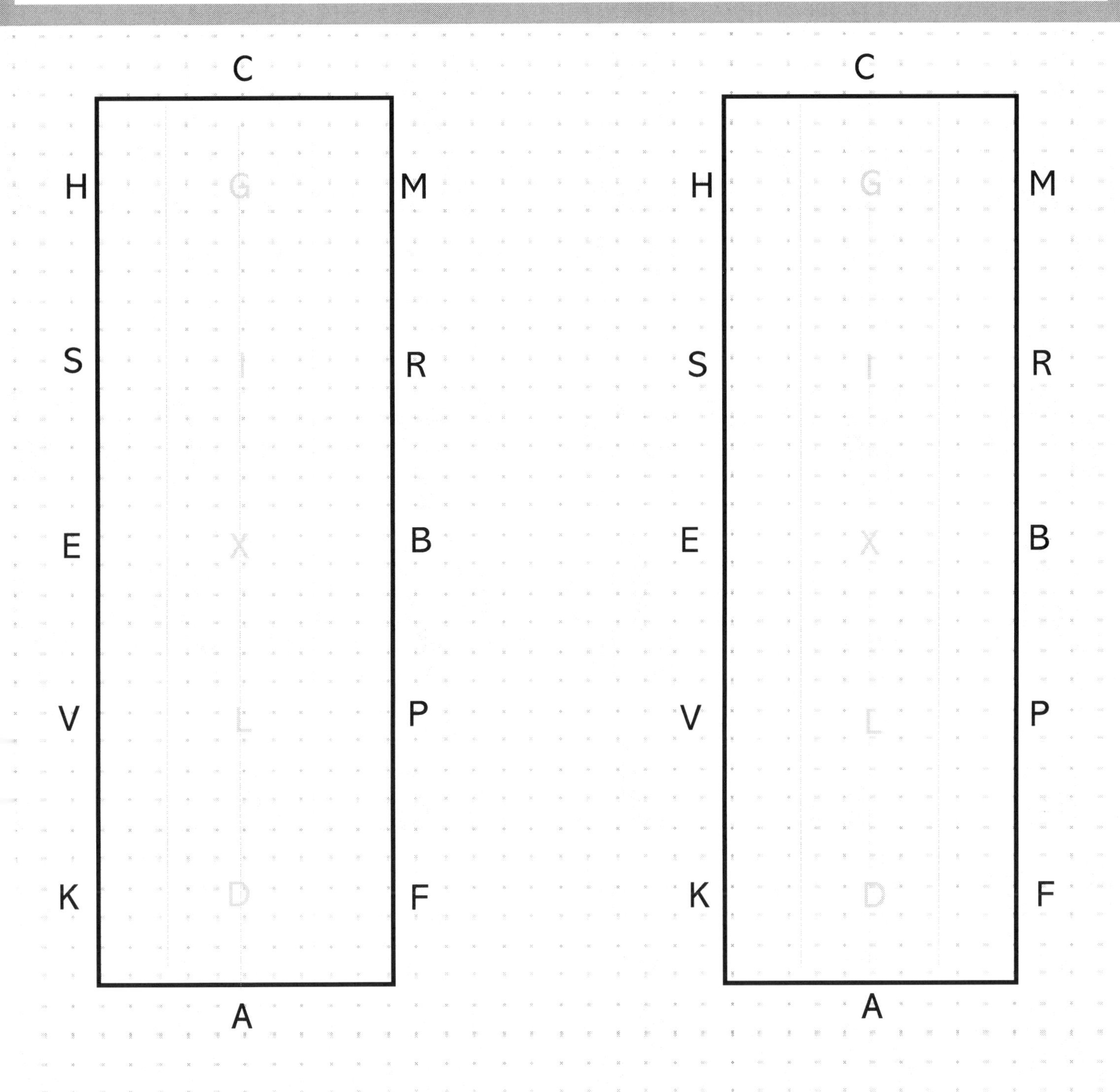

Notes:

Instructor: Date:

Keywords/Visuals

Notes

Lesson Highlights

20 x 60 Meter Dressage Court

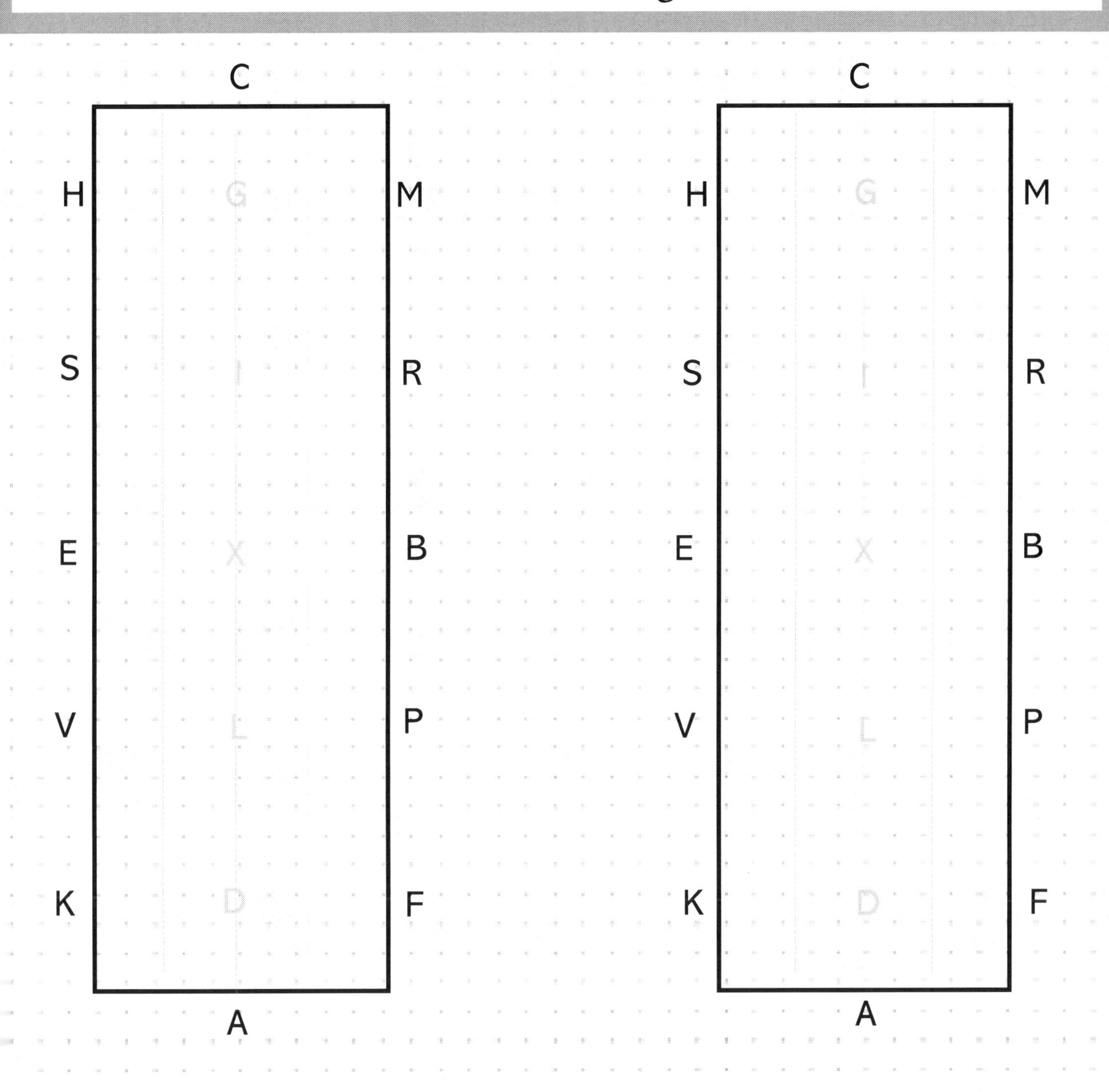

Notes:

Instructor: Date:

Keywords/Visuals

Notes

Lesson Highlights

20 x 60 Meter Dressage Court

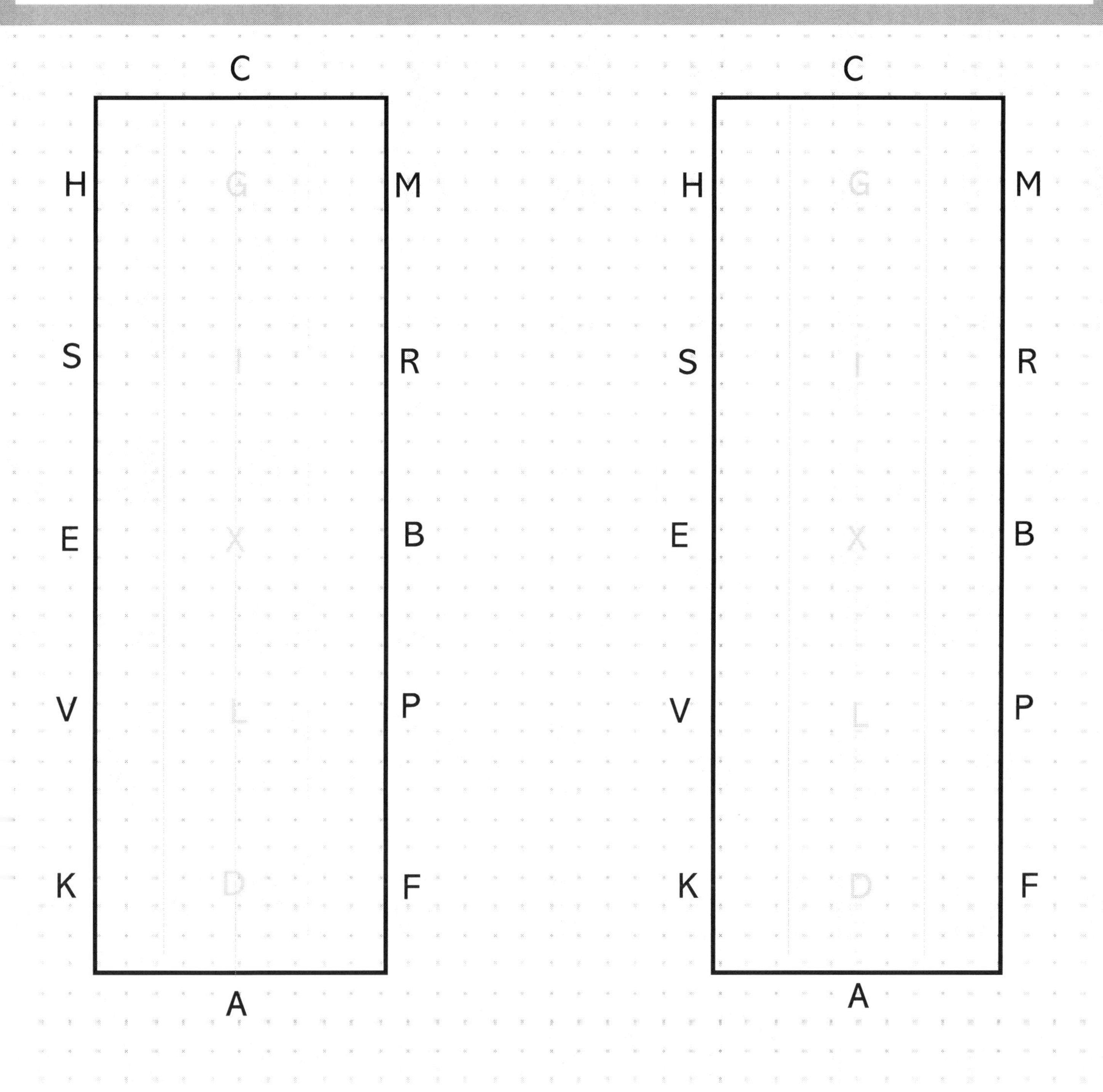

Notes:

Instructor: Date:

Keywords/Visuals

Notes

Lesson Highlights

20 x 60 Meter Dressage Court

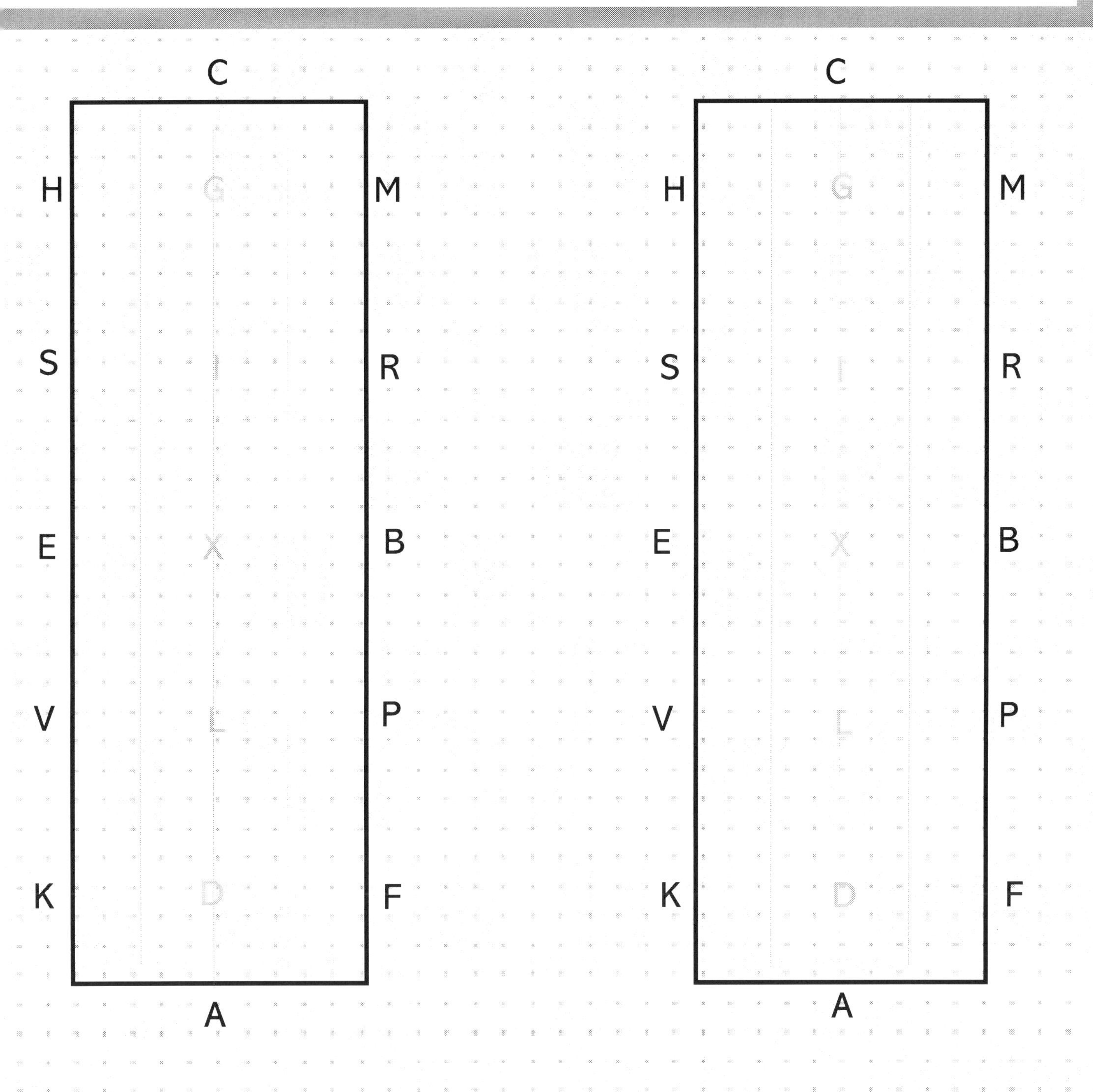

Notes:

Instructor: Date:

Keywords/Visuals

Notes

Lesson Highlights

20 x 60 Meter Dressage Court

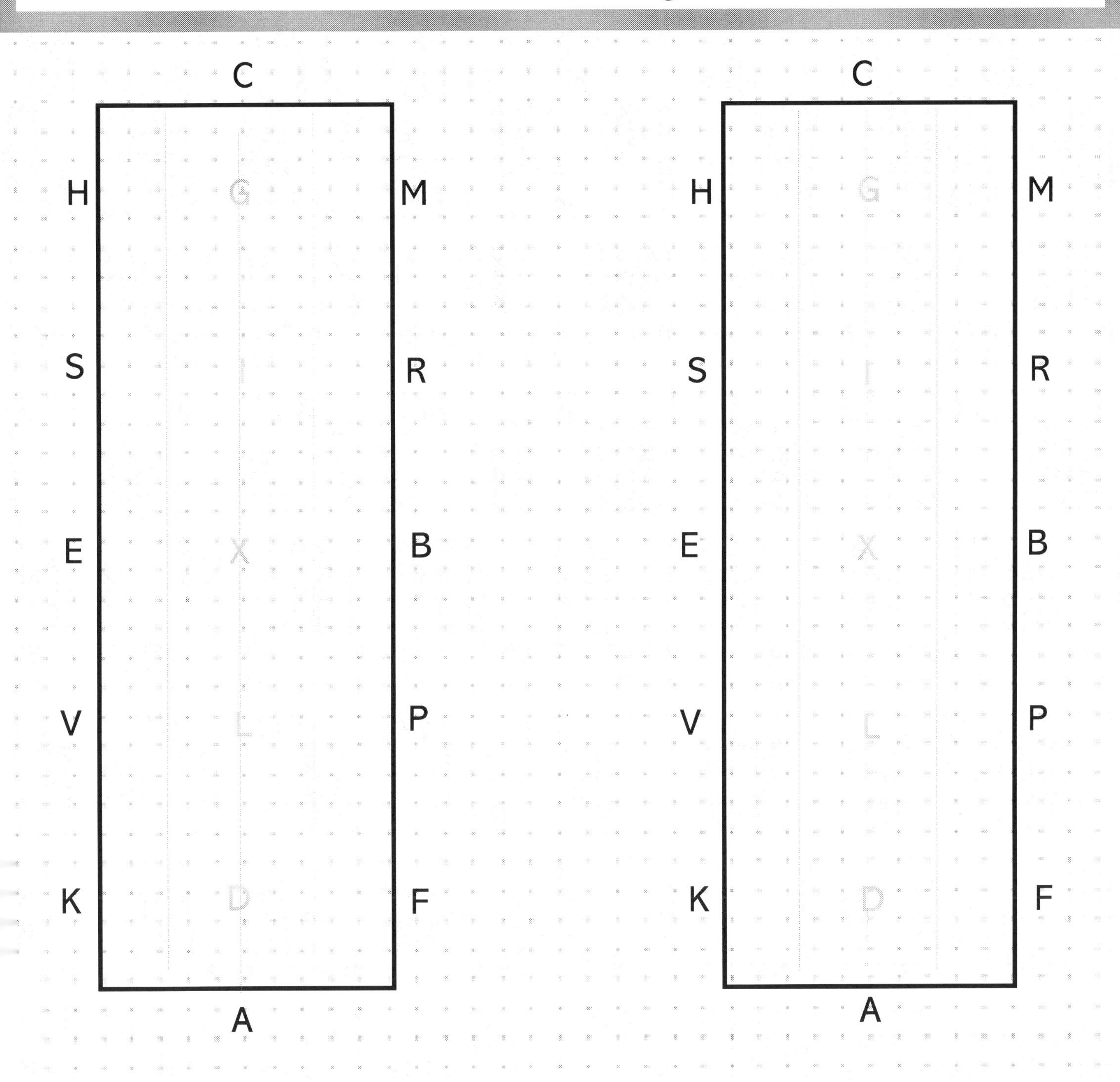

Notes:

Instructor: Date:

Keywords/Visuals

Notes

Lesson Highlights

20 x 60 Meter Dressage Court

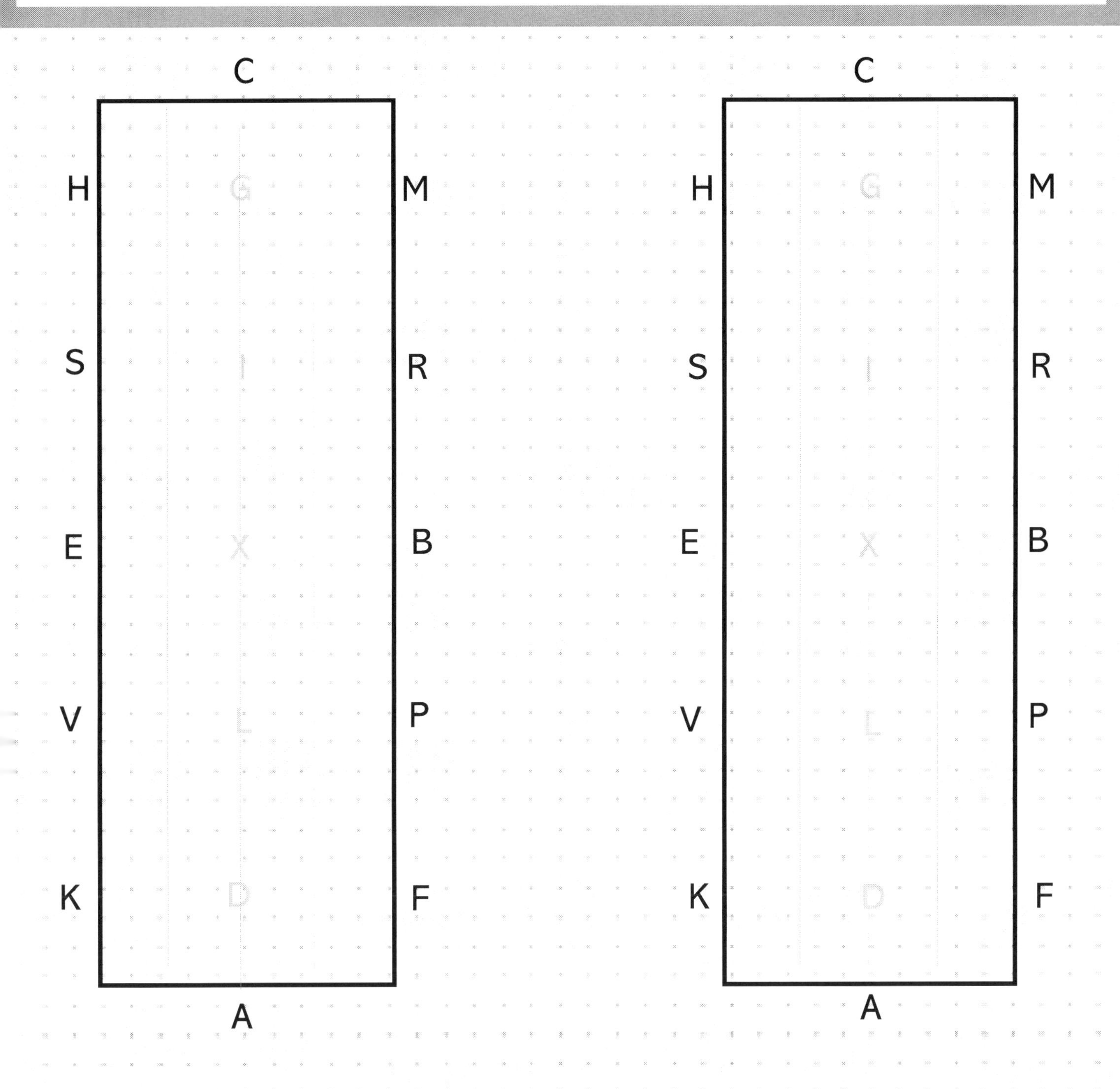

Notes:

Instructor: Date:

Keywords/Visuals	Notes

Lesson Highlights

20 x 60 Meter Dressage Court

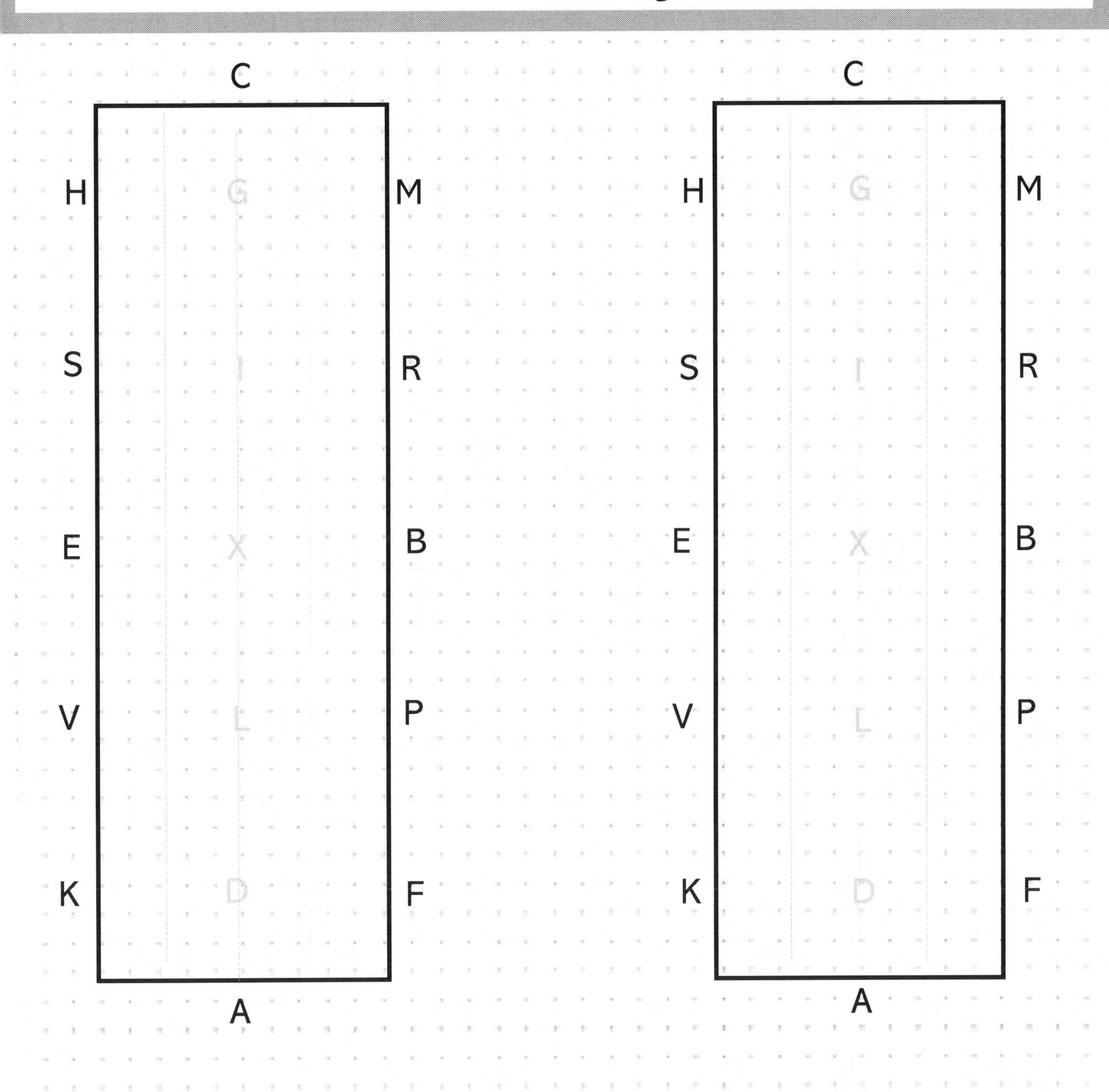

Notes:

Instructor: Date:

Keywords/Visuals

Notes

Lesson Highlights

20 x 60 Meter Dressage Court

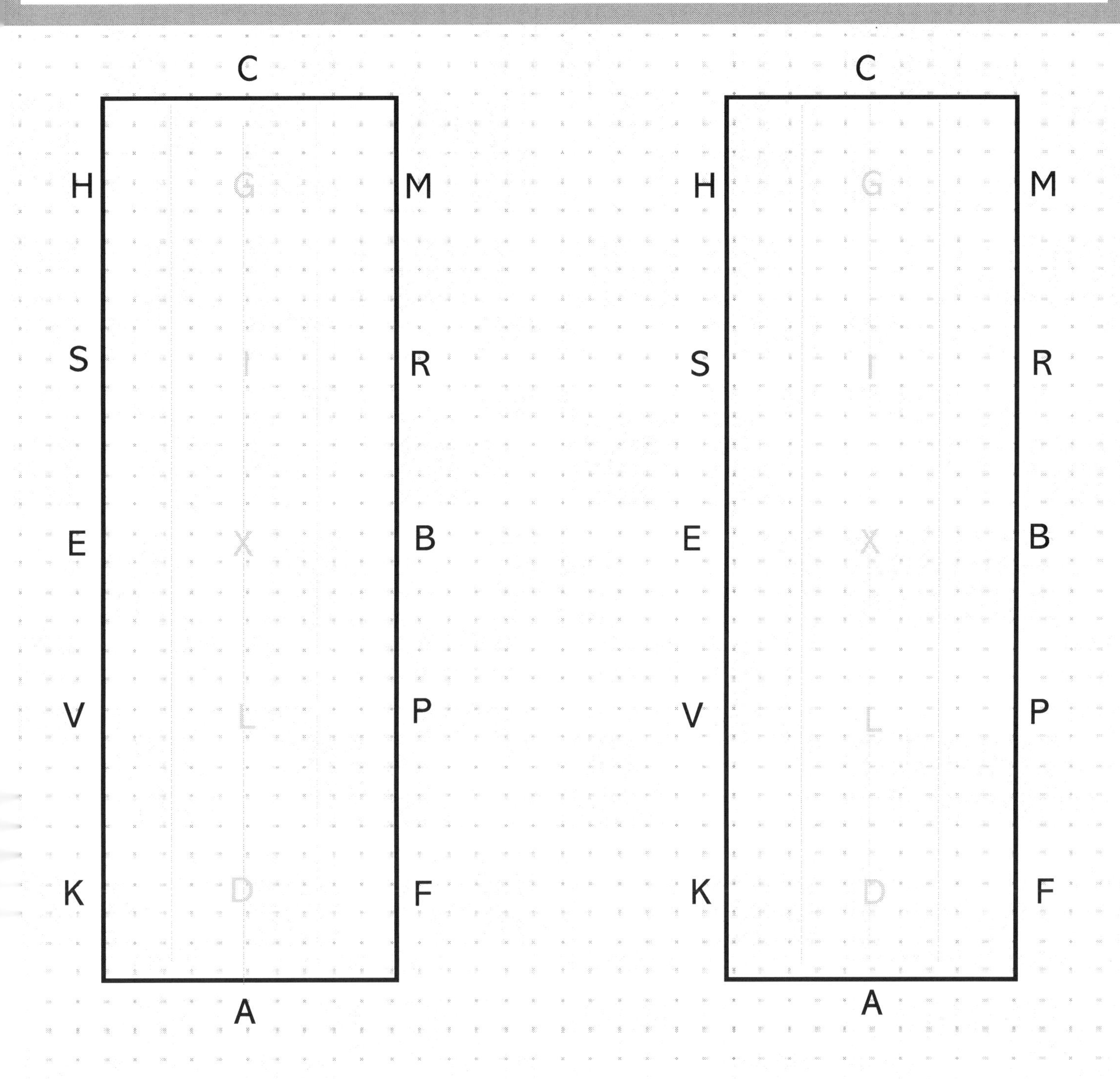

Notes:

Instructor: Date:

Keywords/Visuals	Notes

Lesson Highlights

20 x 60 Meter Dressage Court

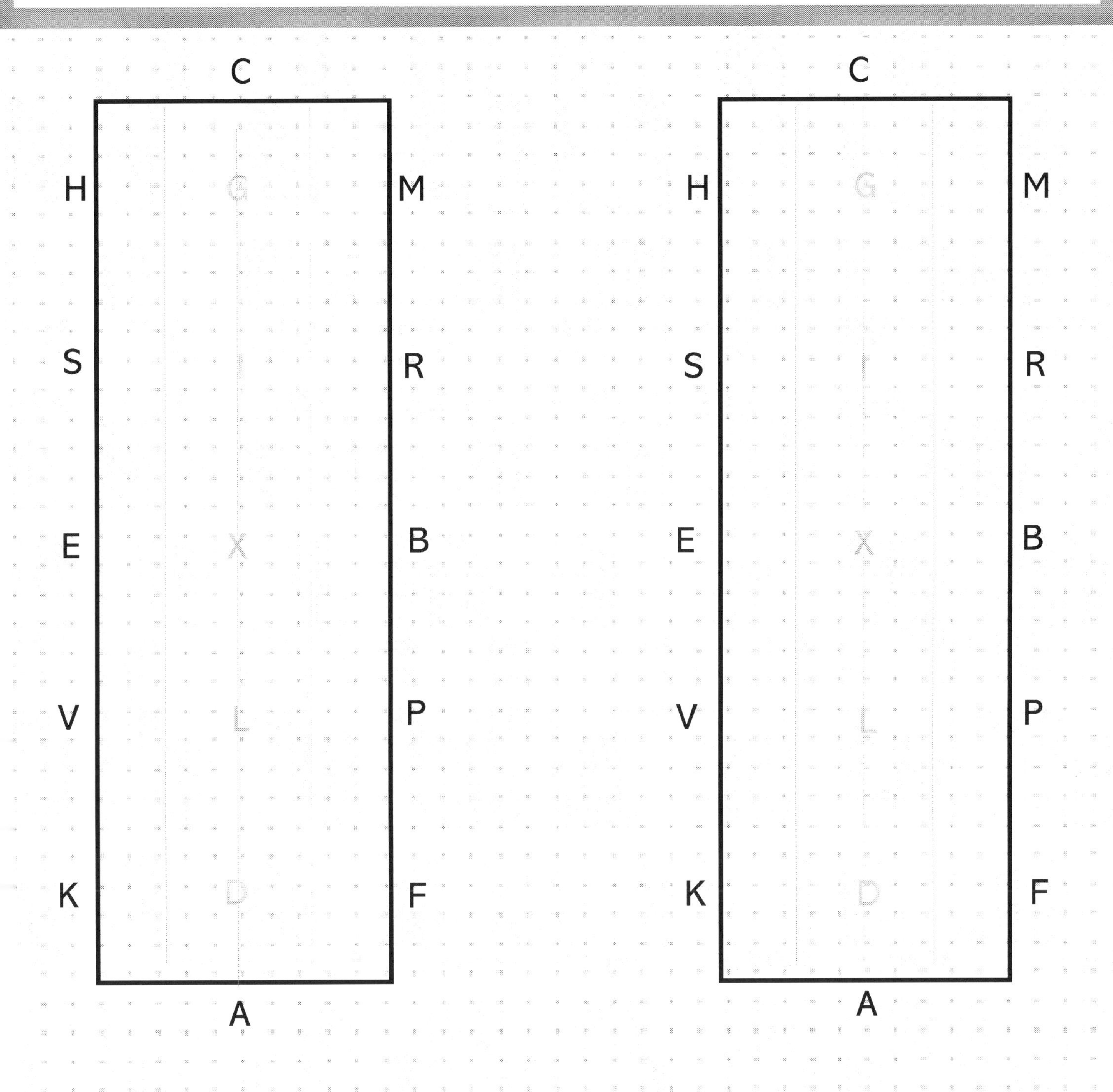

Notes:

Instructor: Date:

Keywords/Visuals

Notes

Lesson Highlights

20 x 60 Meter Dressage Court

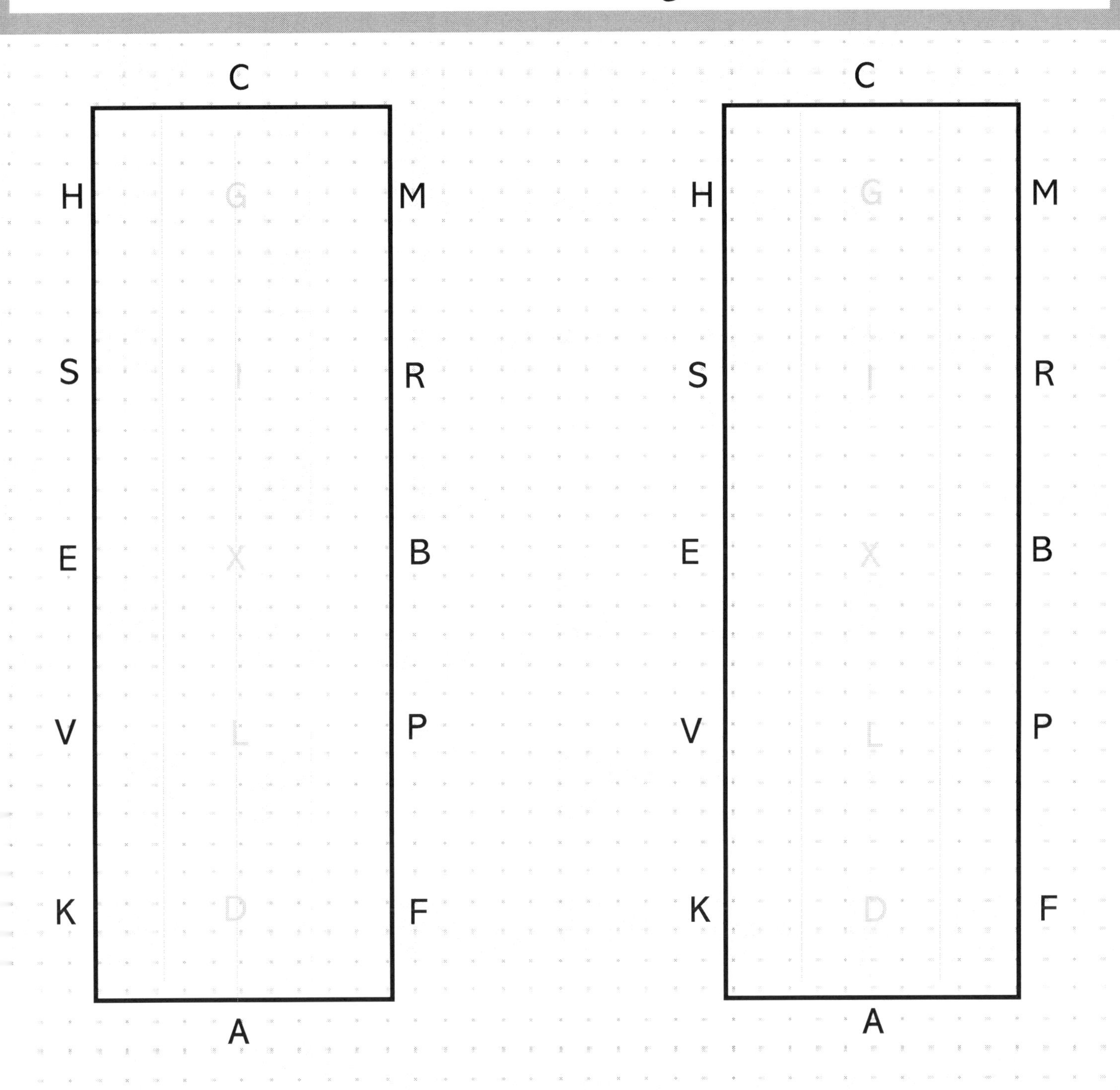

Notes:

Instructor: Date:

Keywords/Visuals

Notes

Lesson Highlights

20 x 60 Meter Dressage Court

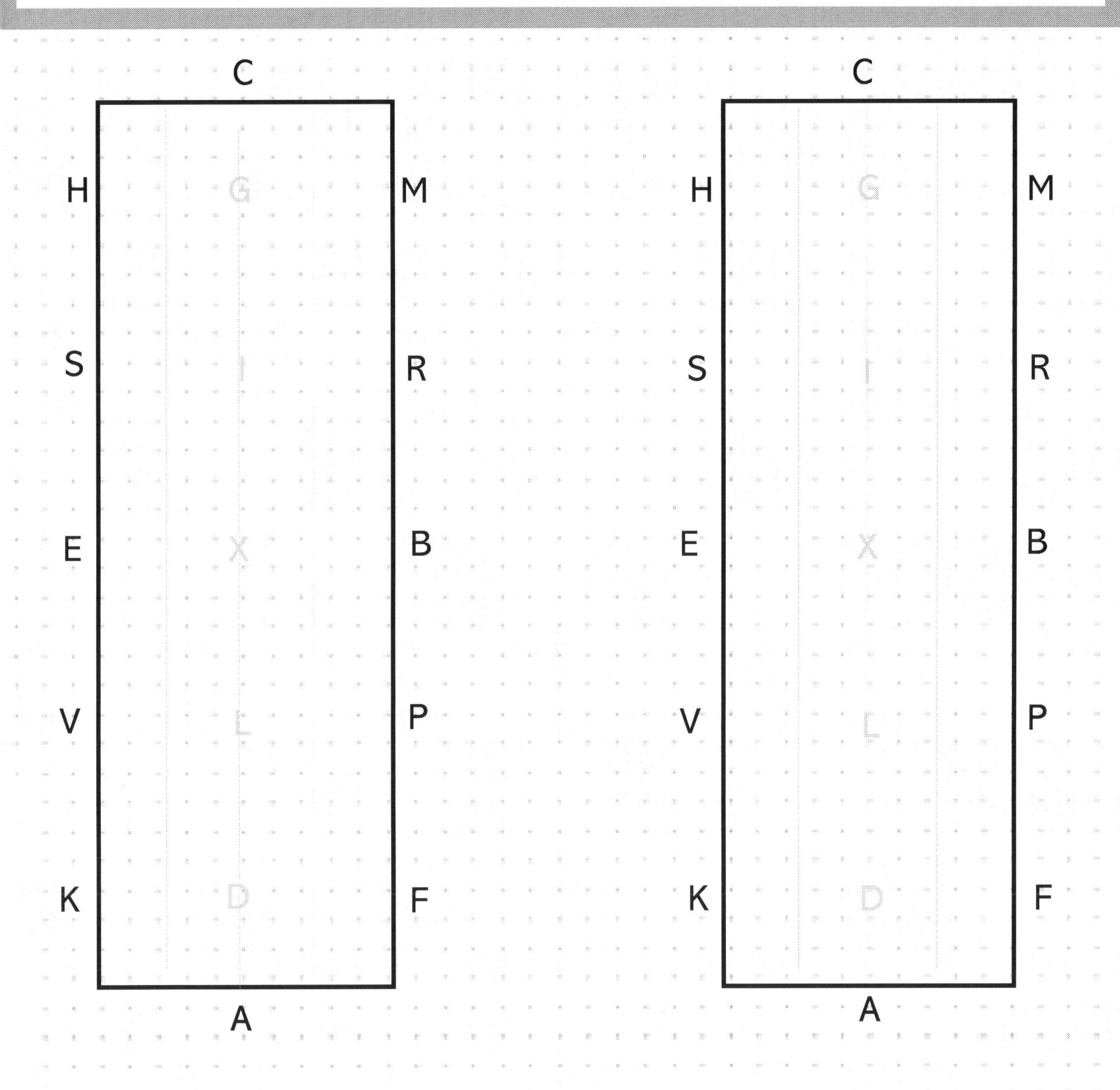

Notes:

Instructor: Date:

Keywords/Visuals	Notes

Lesson Highlights

20 x 60 Meter Dressage Court

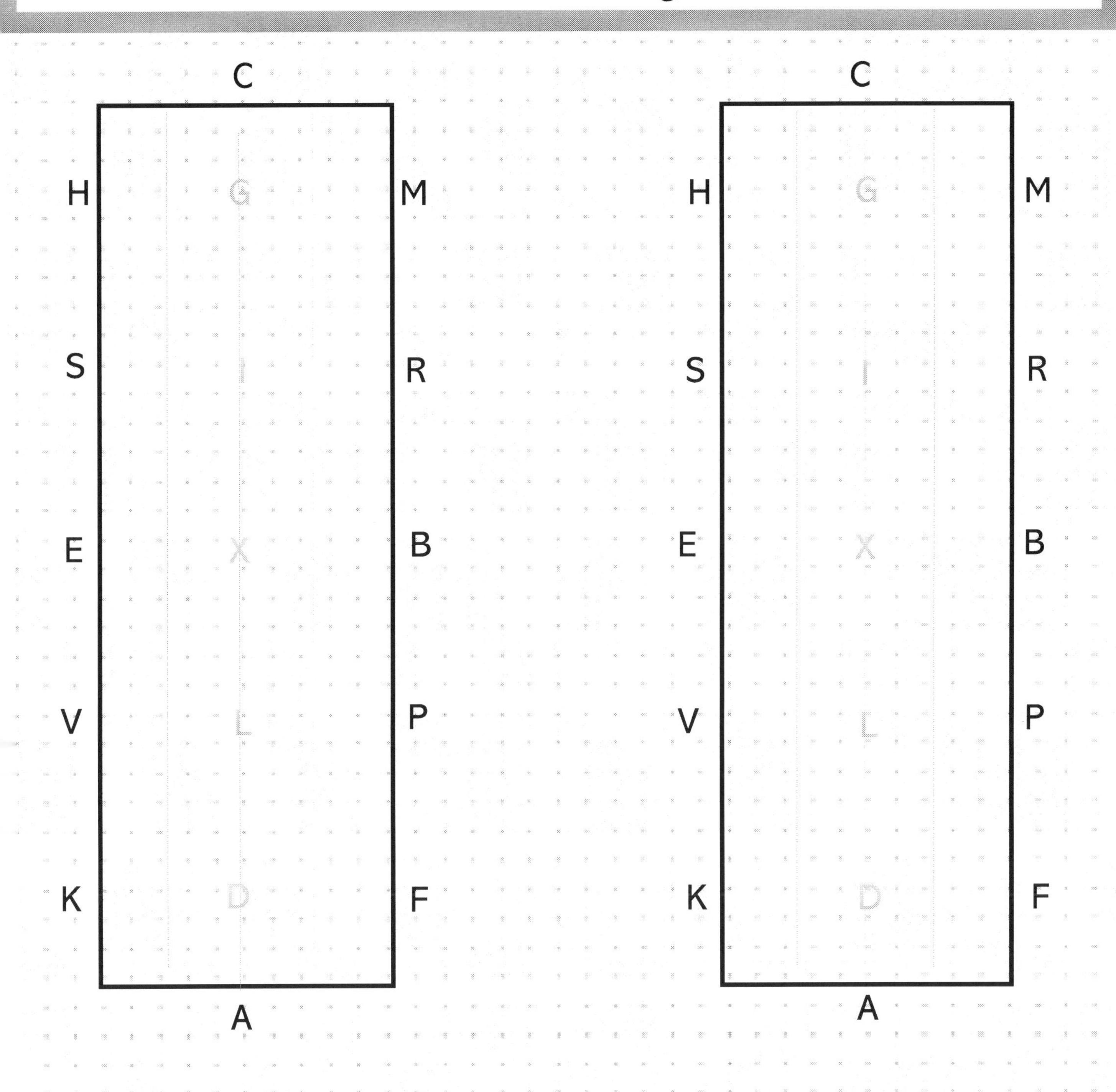

Notes:

Instructor: Date:

Keywords/Visuals	Notes

Lesson Highlights

20 x 60 Meter Dressage Court

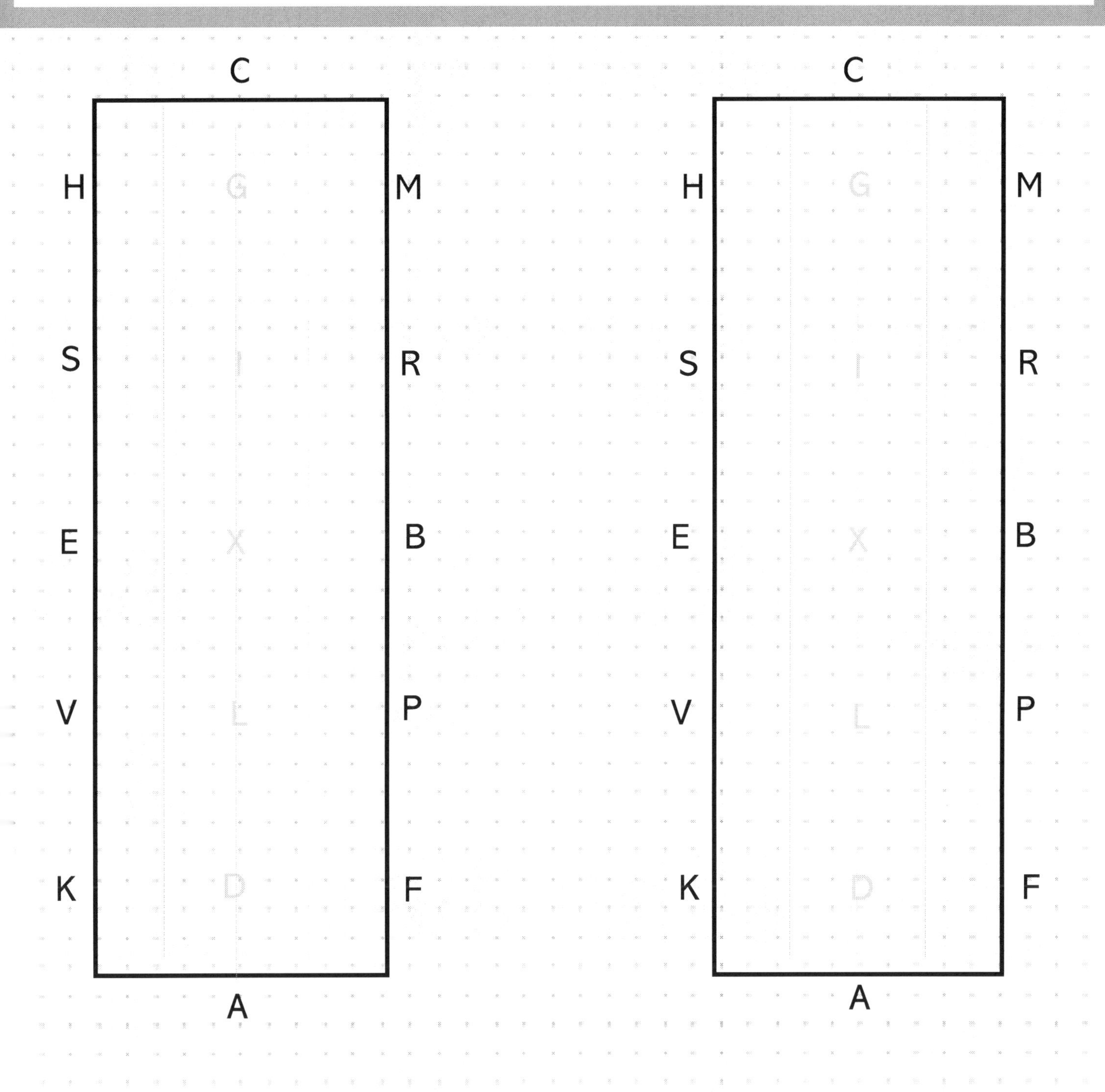

Notes:

Instructor: Date:

Keywords/Visuals

Notes

Lesson Highlights

20 x 60 Meter Dressage Court

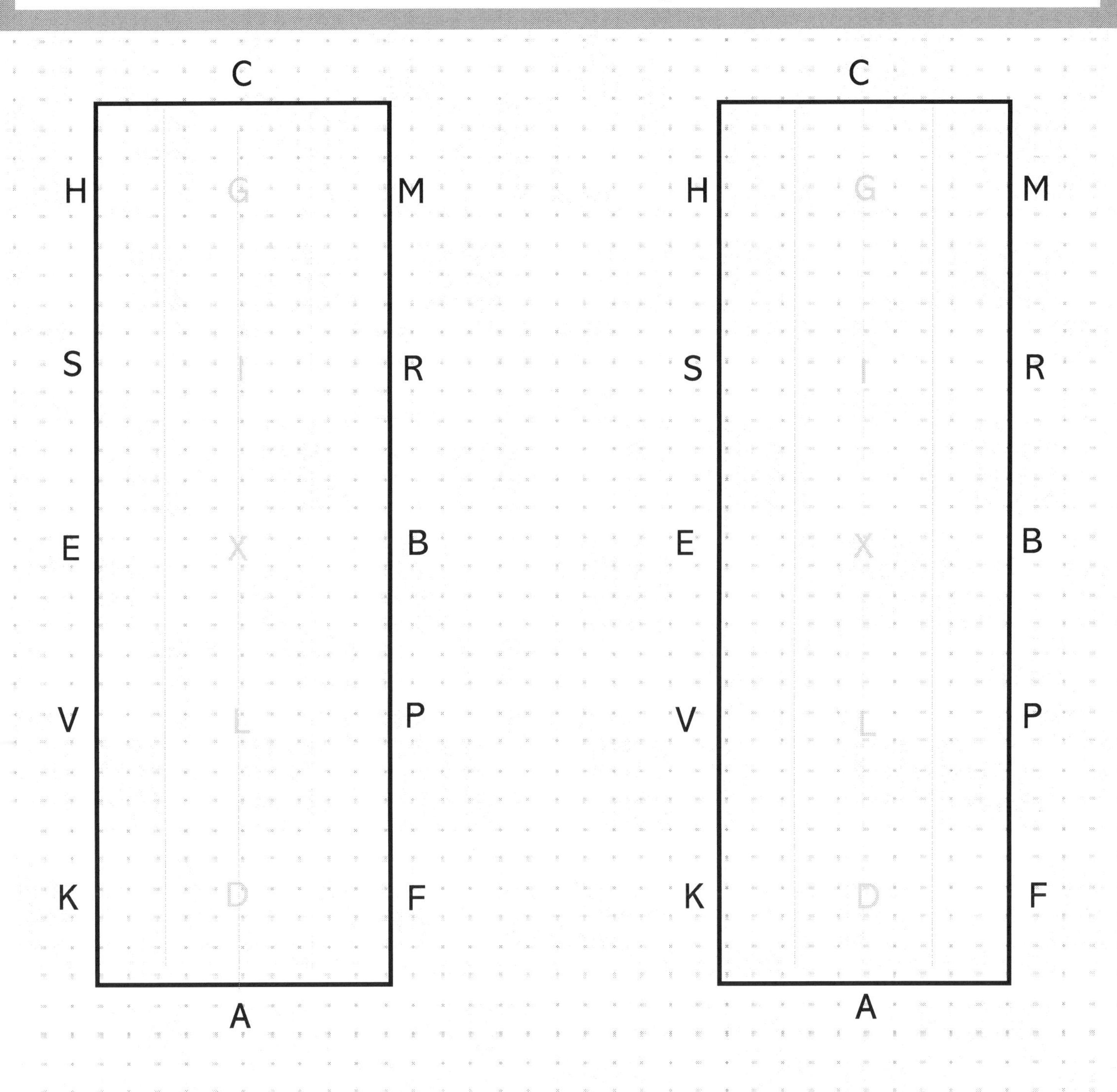

Notes:

Instructor: Date:

Keywords/Visuals

Notes

Lesson Highlights

20 x 60 Meter Dressage Court

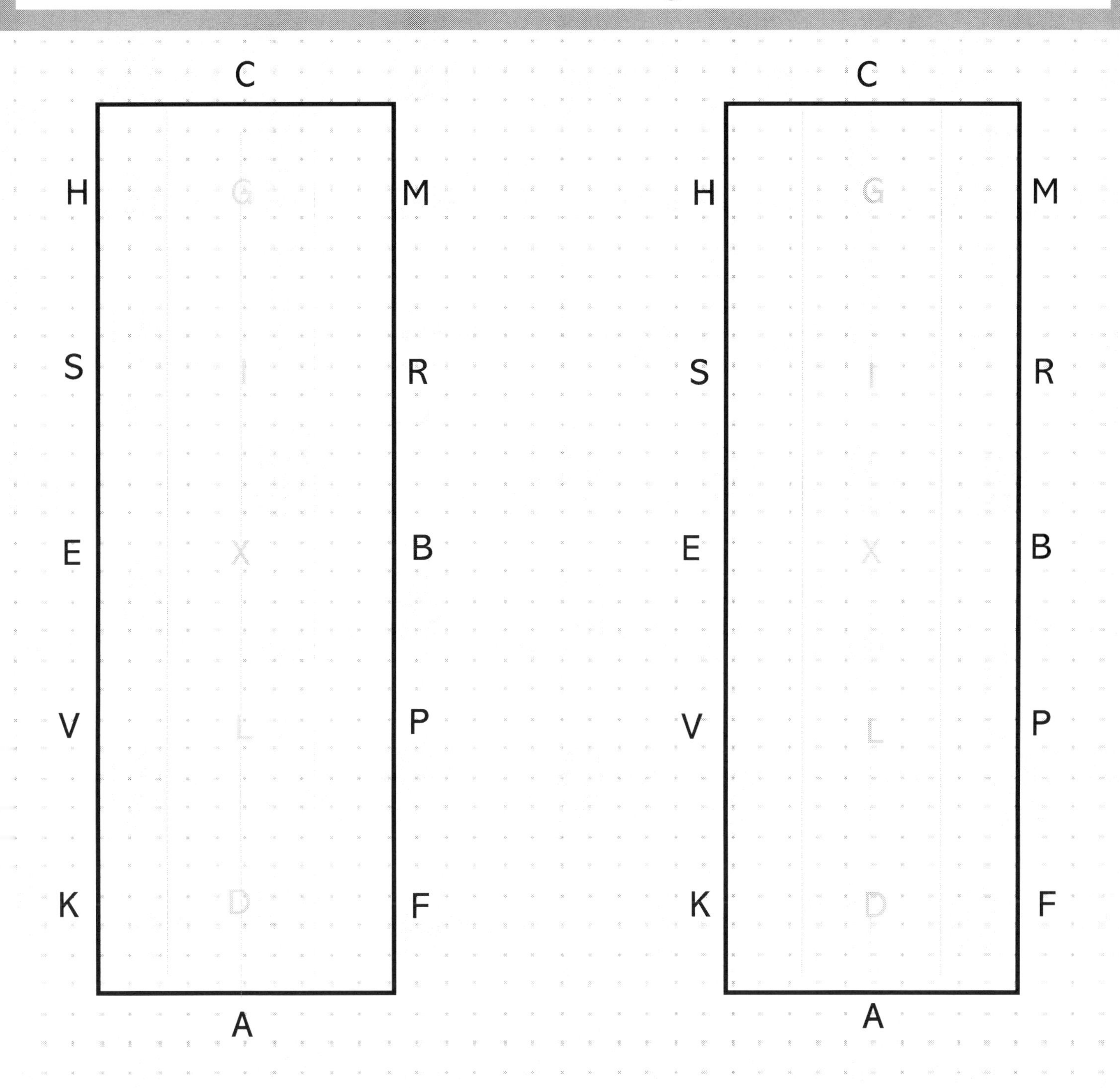

Notes:

Instructor: Date:

Keywords/Visuals

Notes

Lesson Highlights

20 x 60 Meter Dressage Court

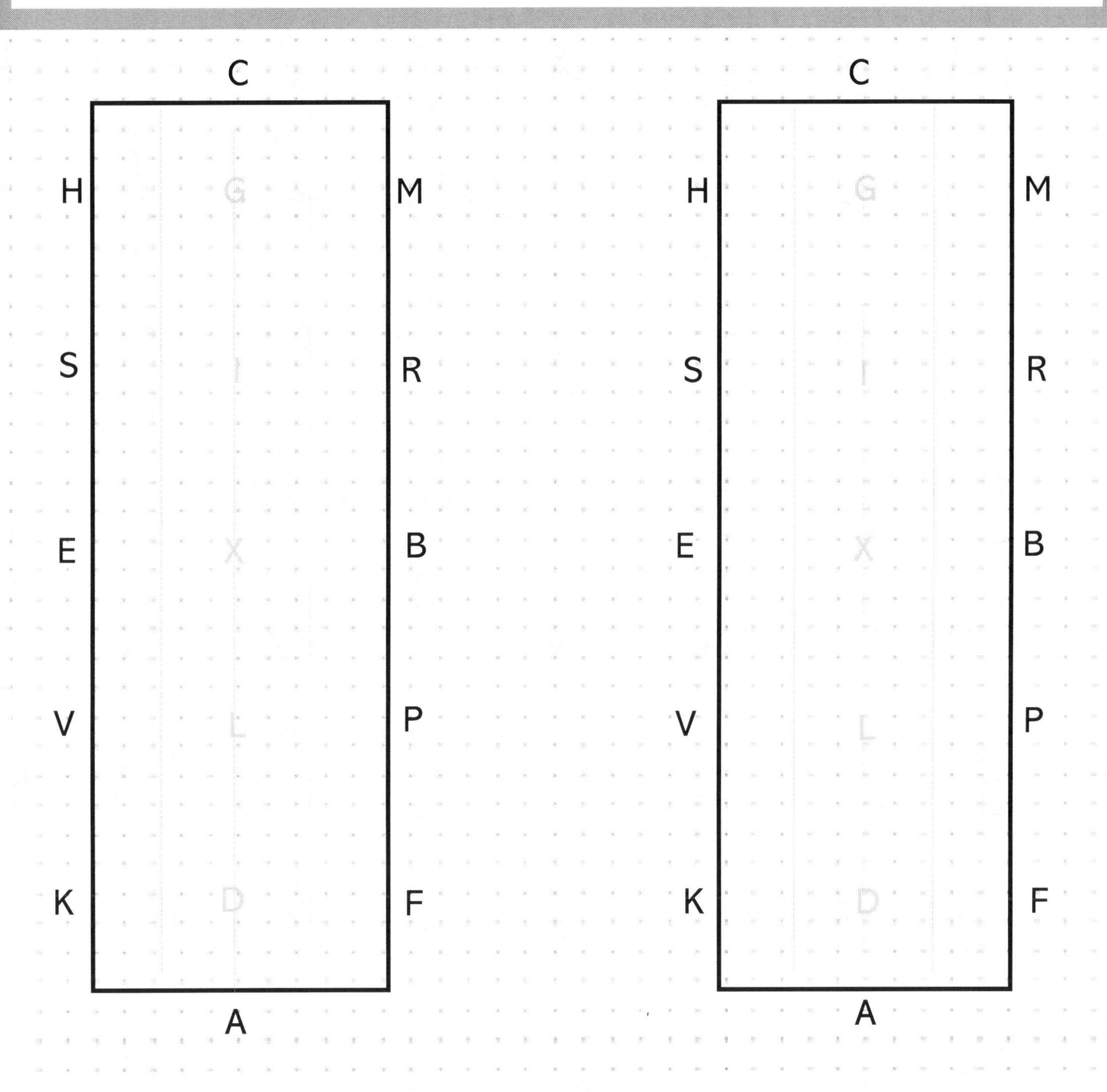

Notes:

Instructor: Date:

Keywords/Visuals

Notes

Lesson Highlights

20 x 60 Meter Dressage Court

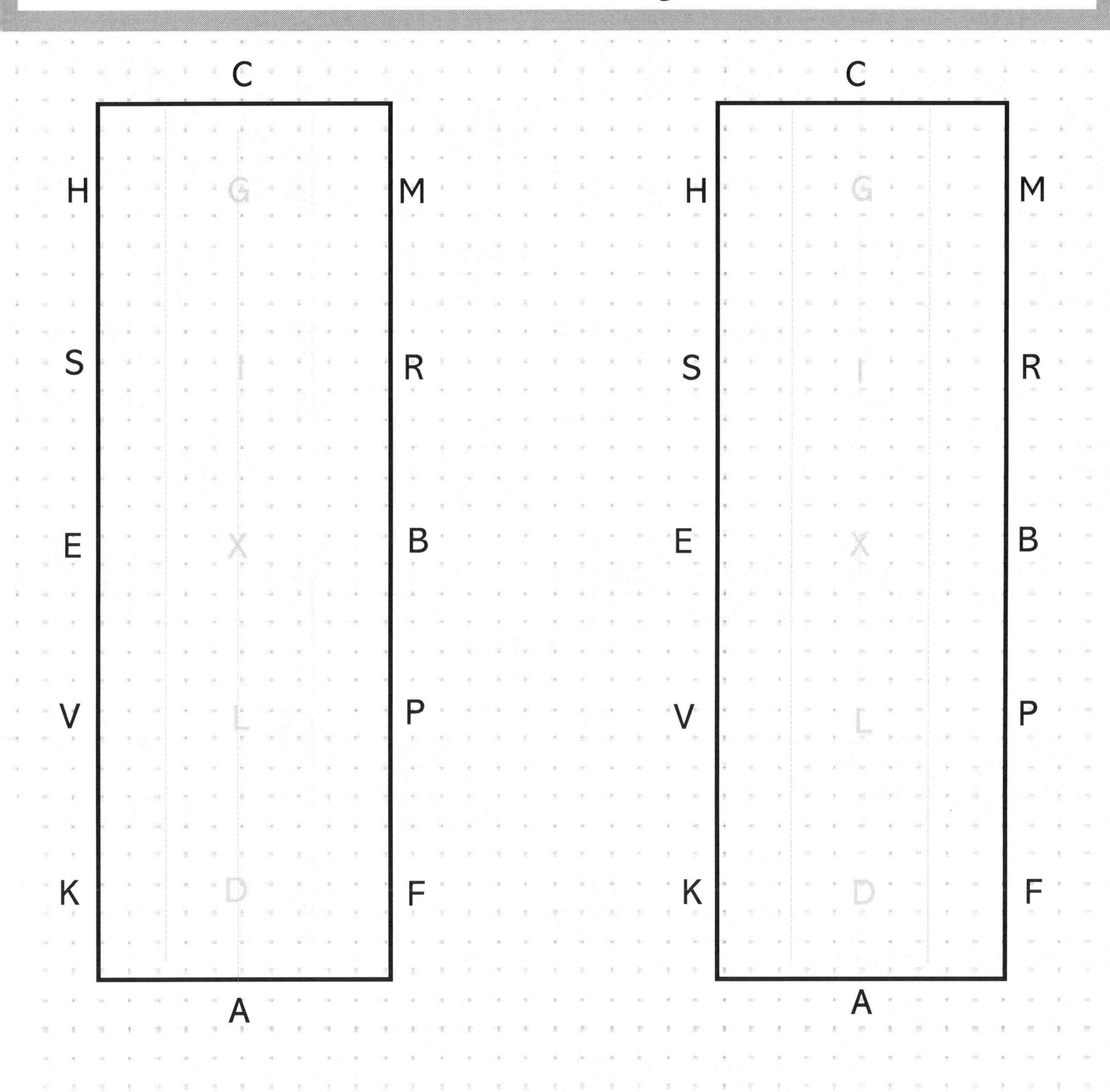

Notes:

Instructor: Date:

Keywords/Visuals

Notes

Lesson Highlights

20 x 60 Meter Dressage Court

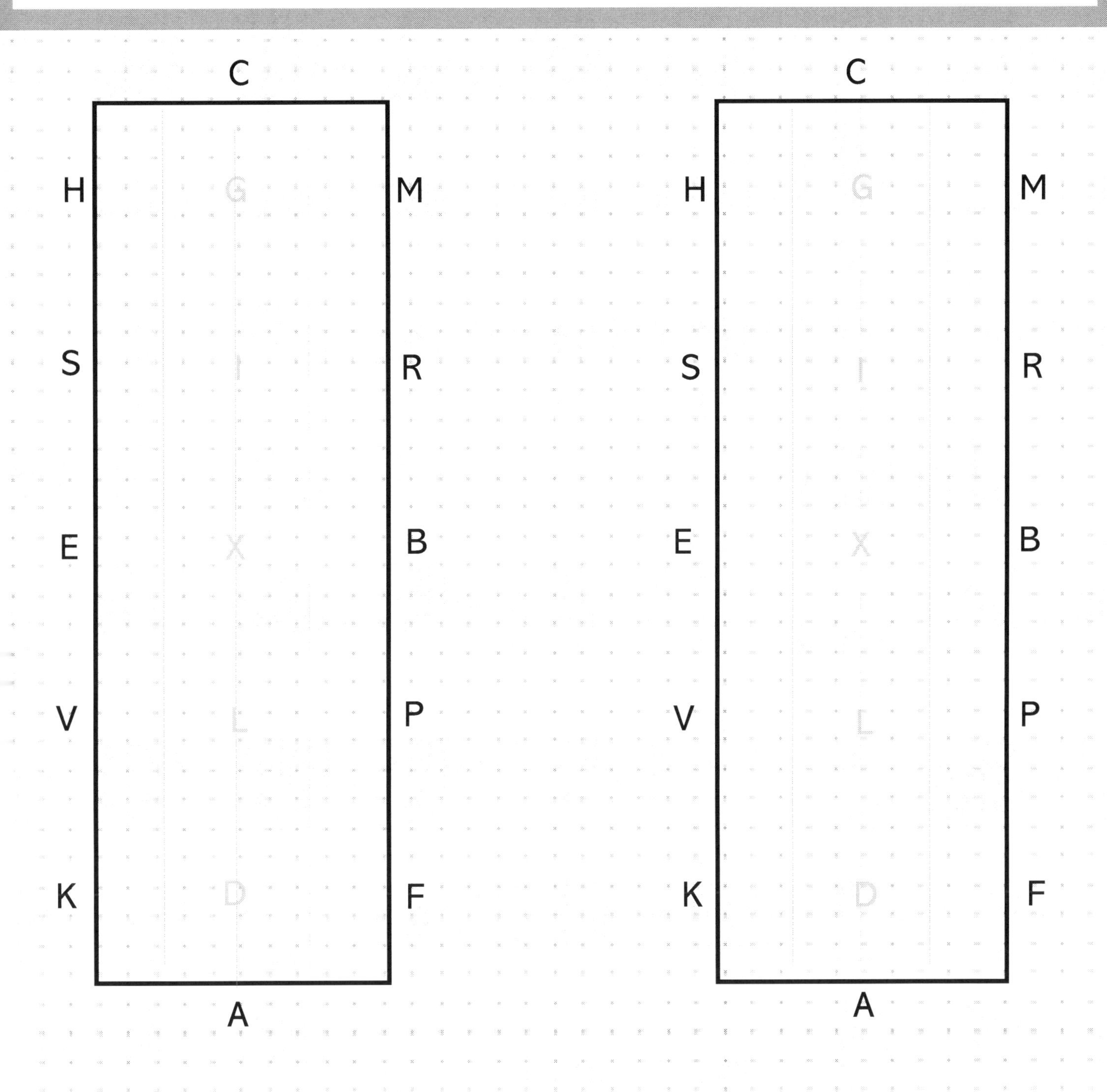

Notes:

Instructor: Date:

Keywords/Visuals	Notes

Lesson Highlights

20 x 60 Meter Dressage Court

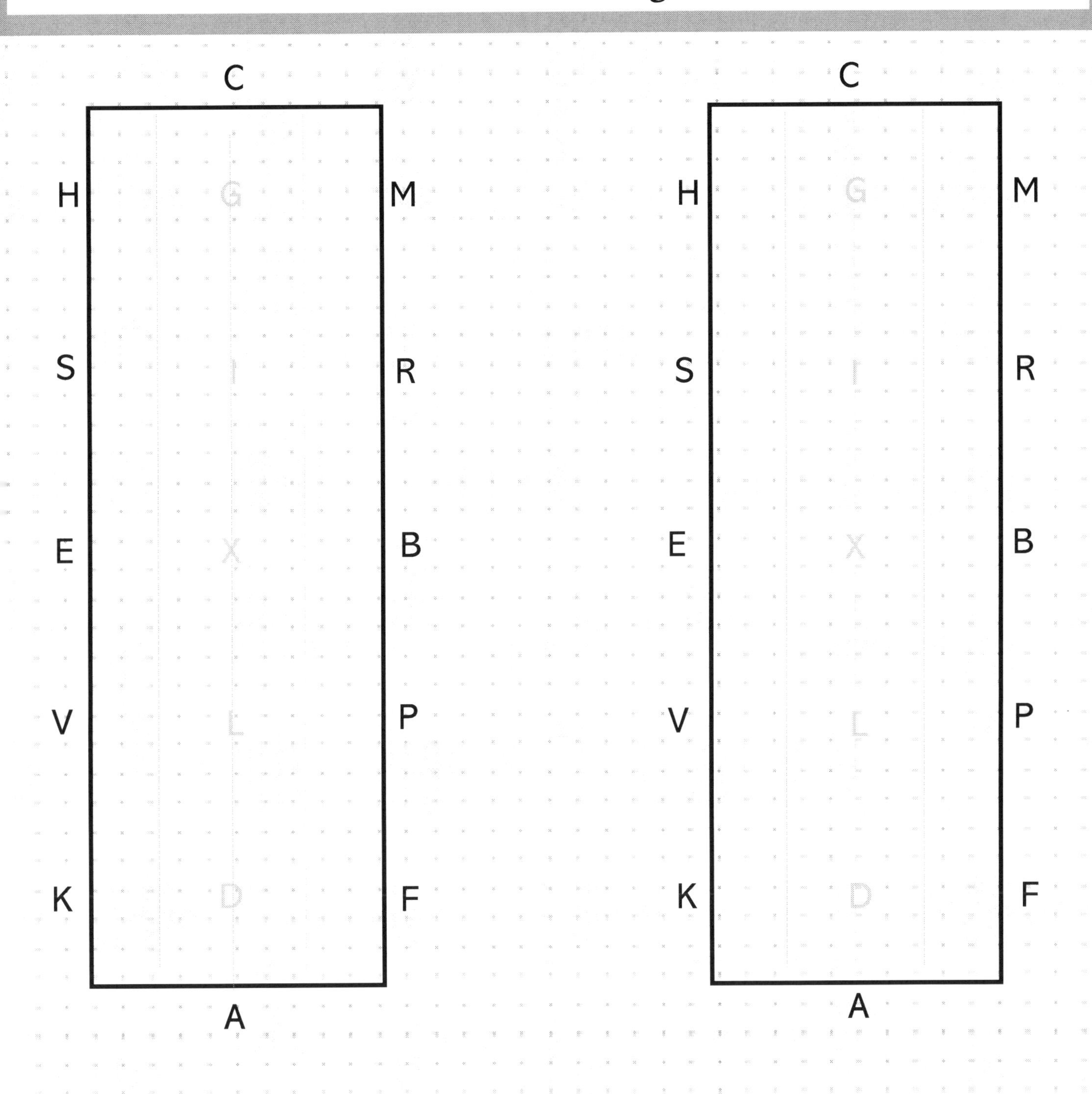

Notes:

Instructor: Date:

Keywords/Visuals

Notes

Lesson Highlights

20 x 60 Meter Dressage Court

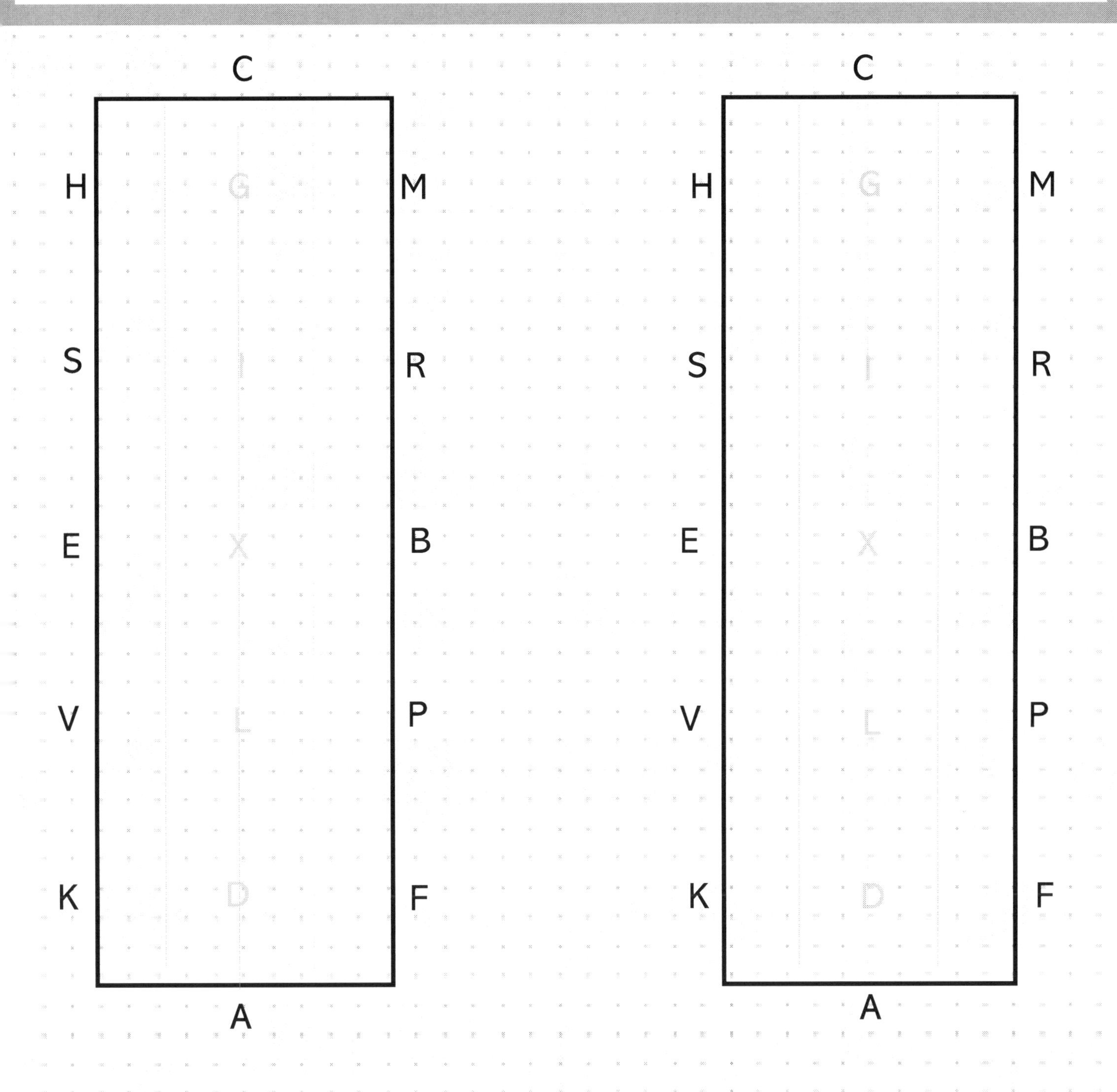

Notes:

Instructor: Date:

Keywords/Visuals

Notes

Lesson Highlights

20 x 60 Meter Dressage Court

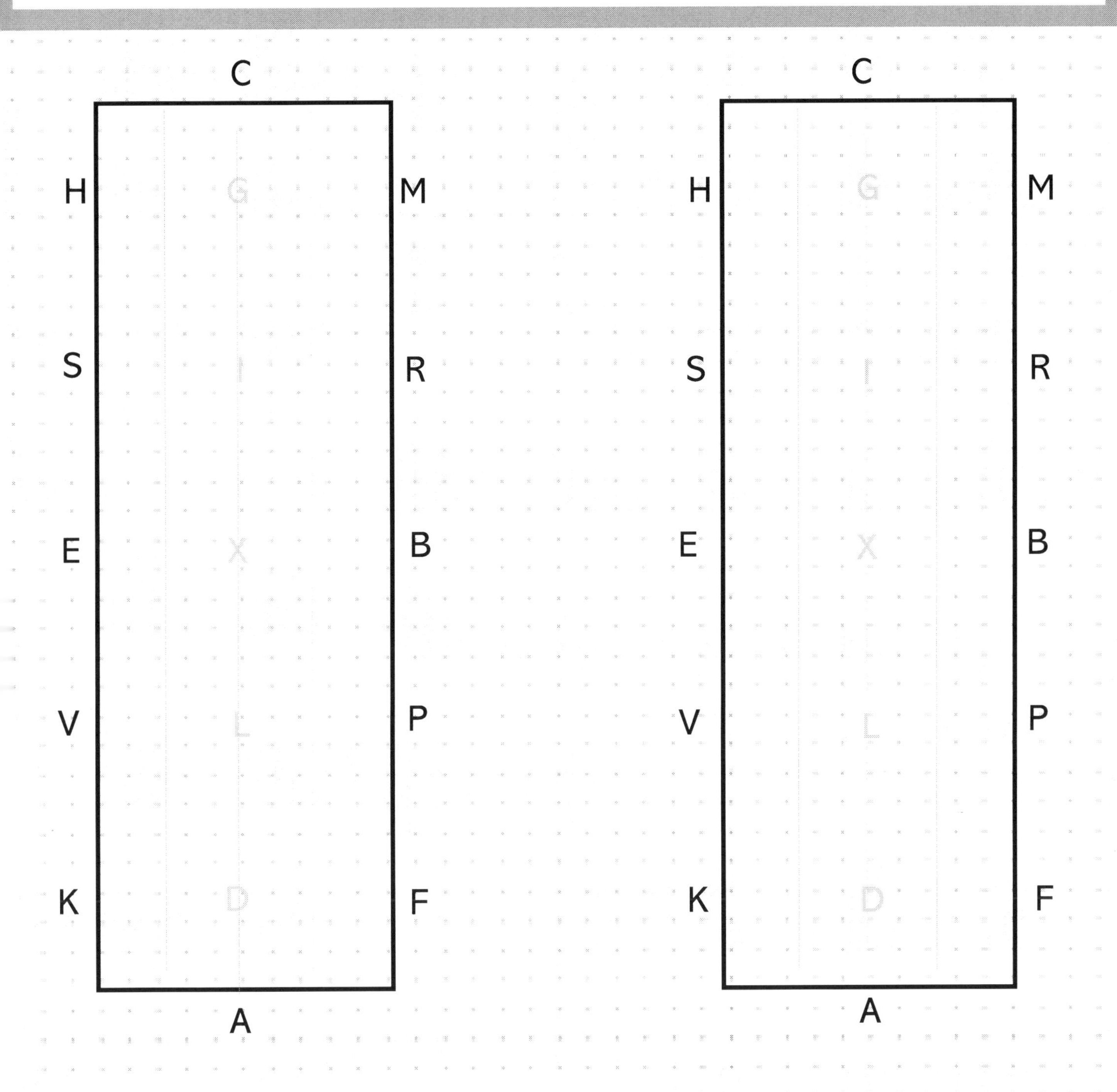

Notes:

Instructor: Date:

Keywords/Visuals

Notes

Lesson Highlights

20 x 60 Meter Dressage Court

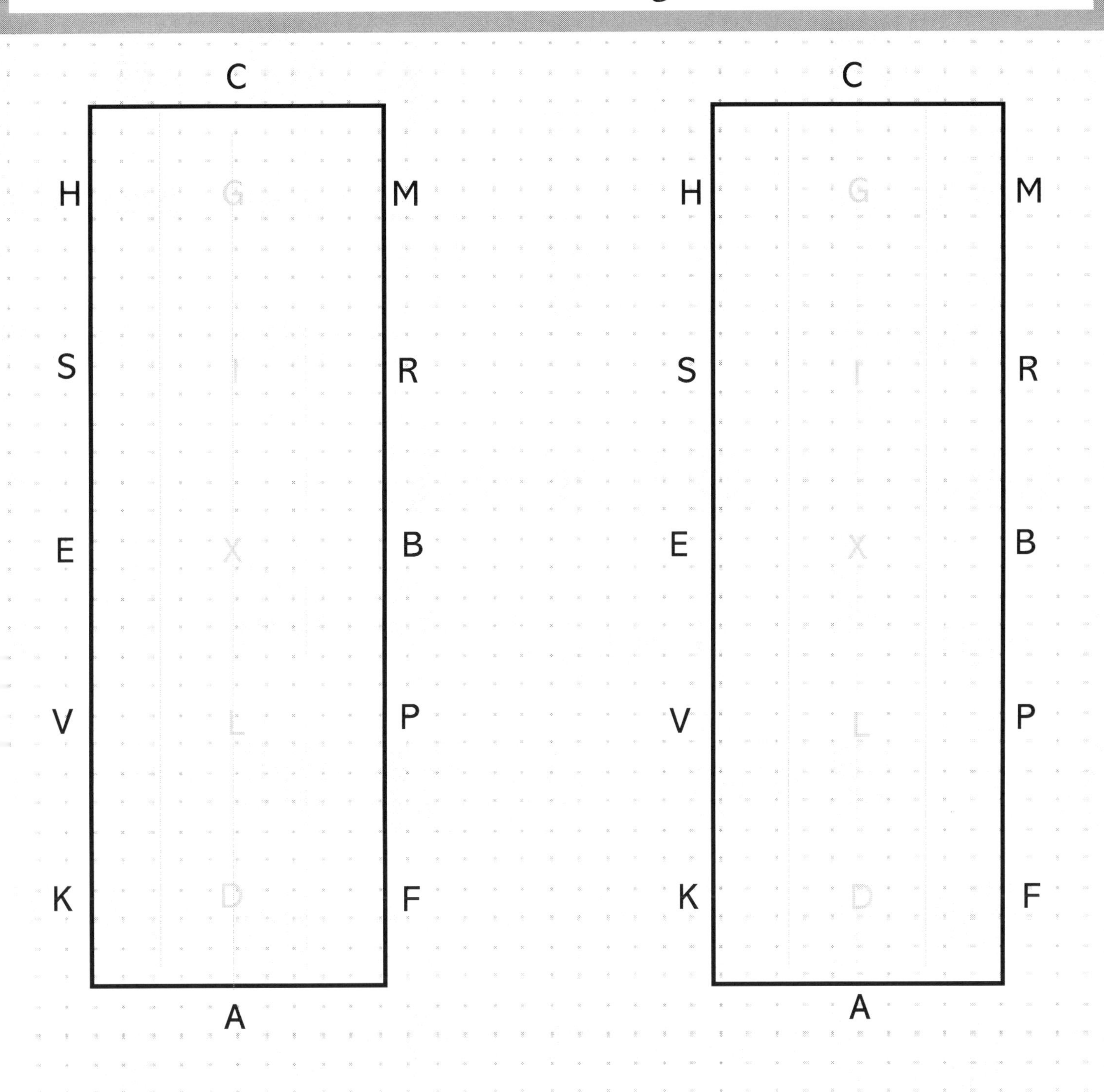

Notes:

Instructor: Date:

Keywords/Visuals

Notes

Lesson Highlights

20 x 60 Meter Dressage Court

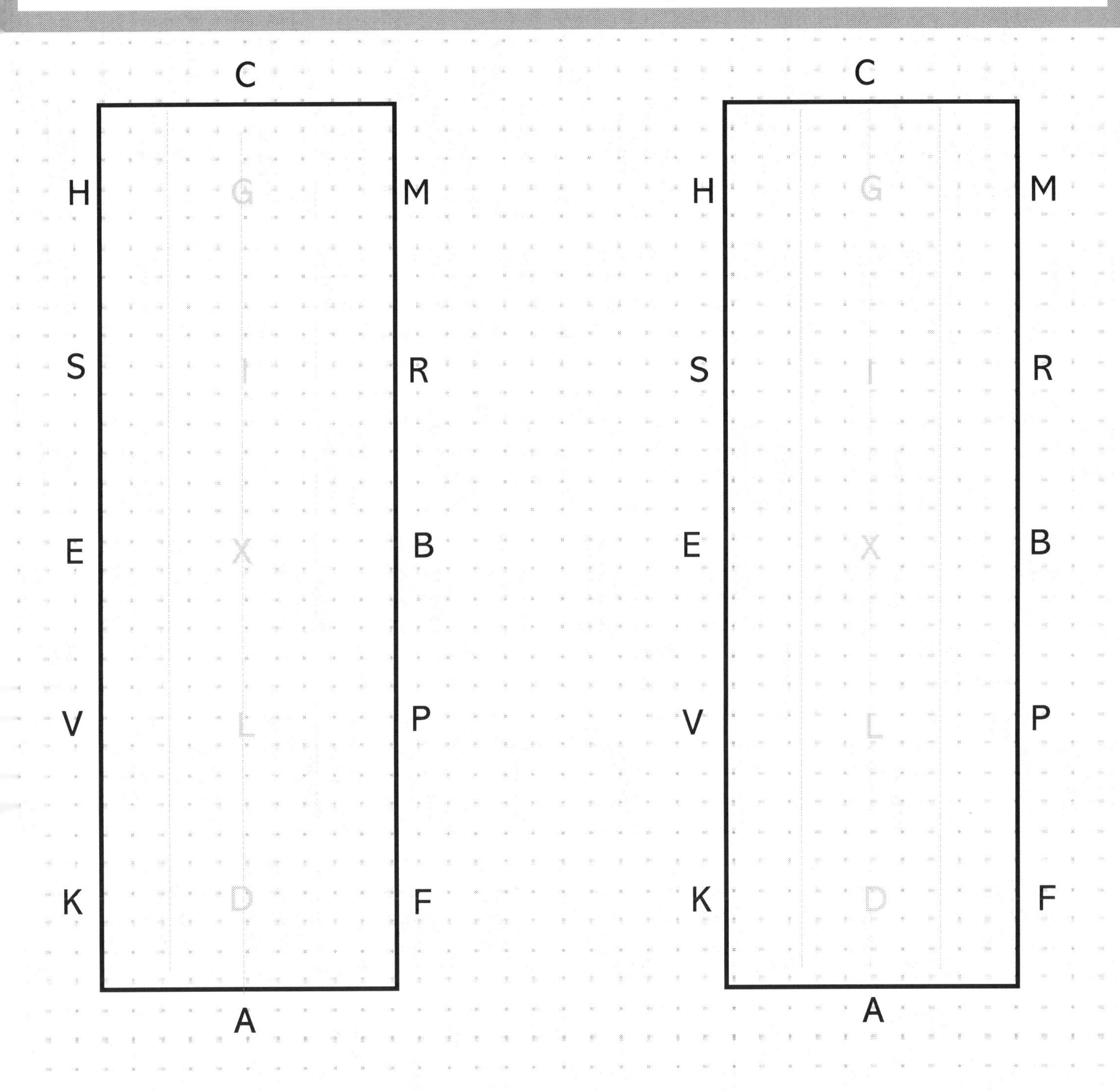

Notes:

Instructor: Date:

Keywords/Visuals

Notes

Lesson Highlights

20 x 60 Meter Dressage Court

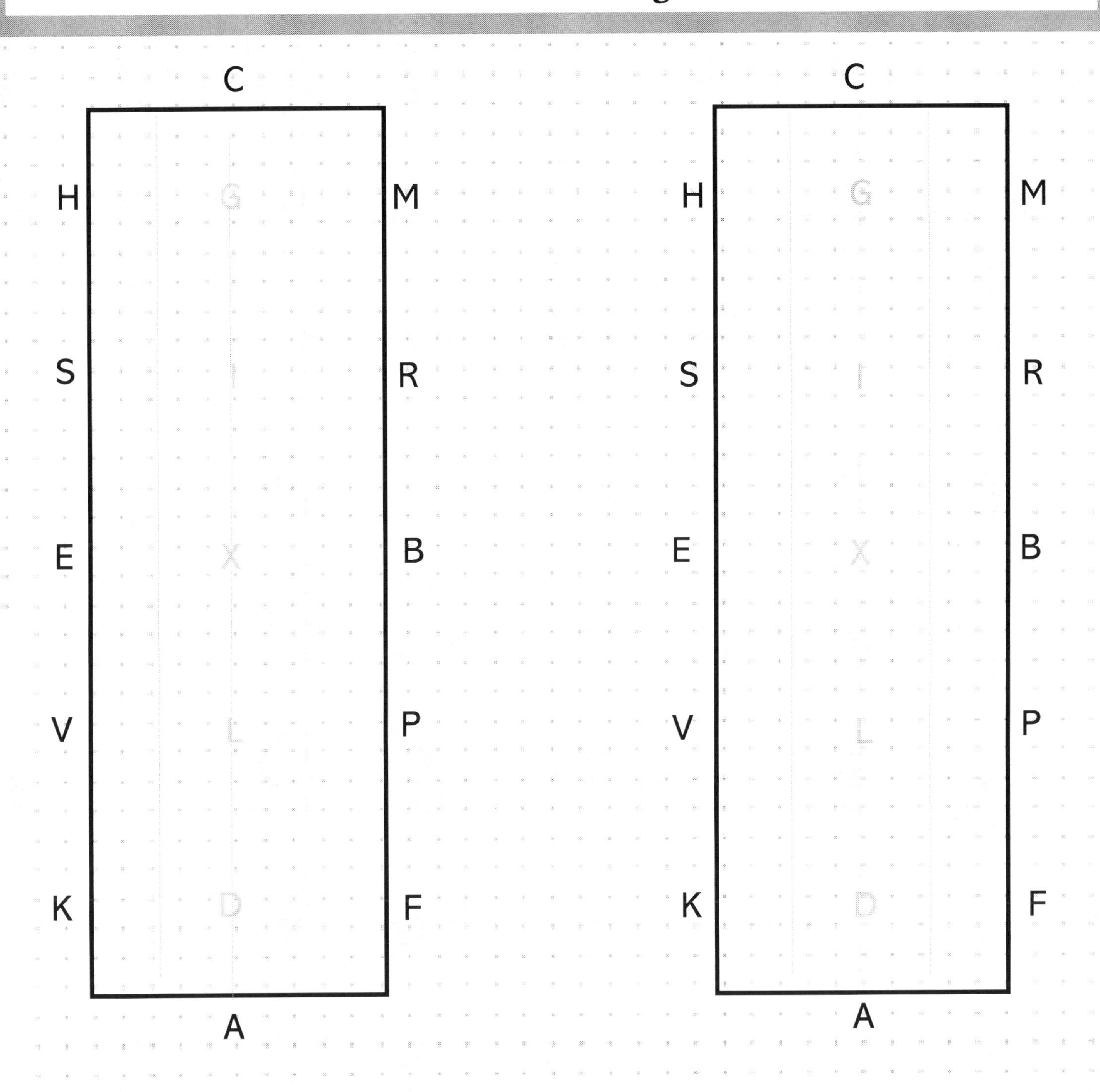

Notes:

Instructor: Date:

Keywords/Visuals

Notes

Lesson Highlights

20 x 60 Meter Dressage Court

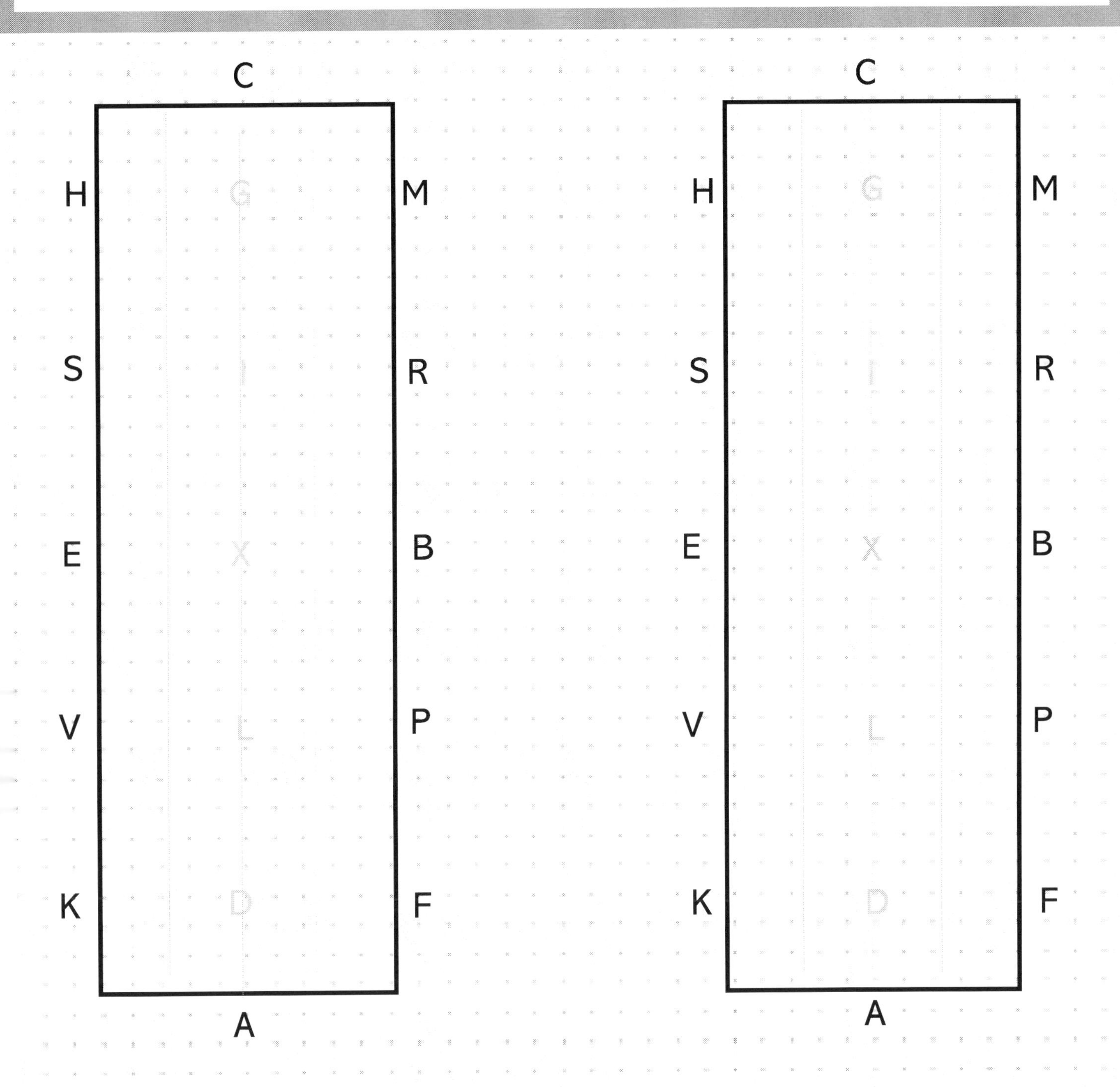

Notes:

Instructor: Date:

Keywords/Visuals

Notes

Lesson Highlights

20 x 60 Meter Dressage Court

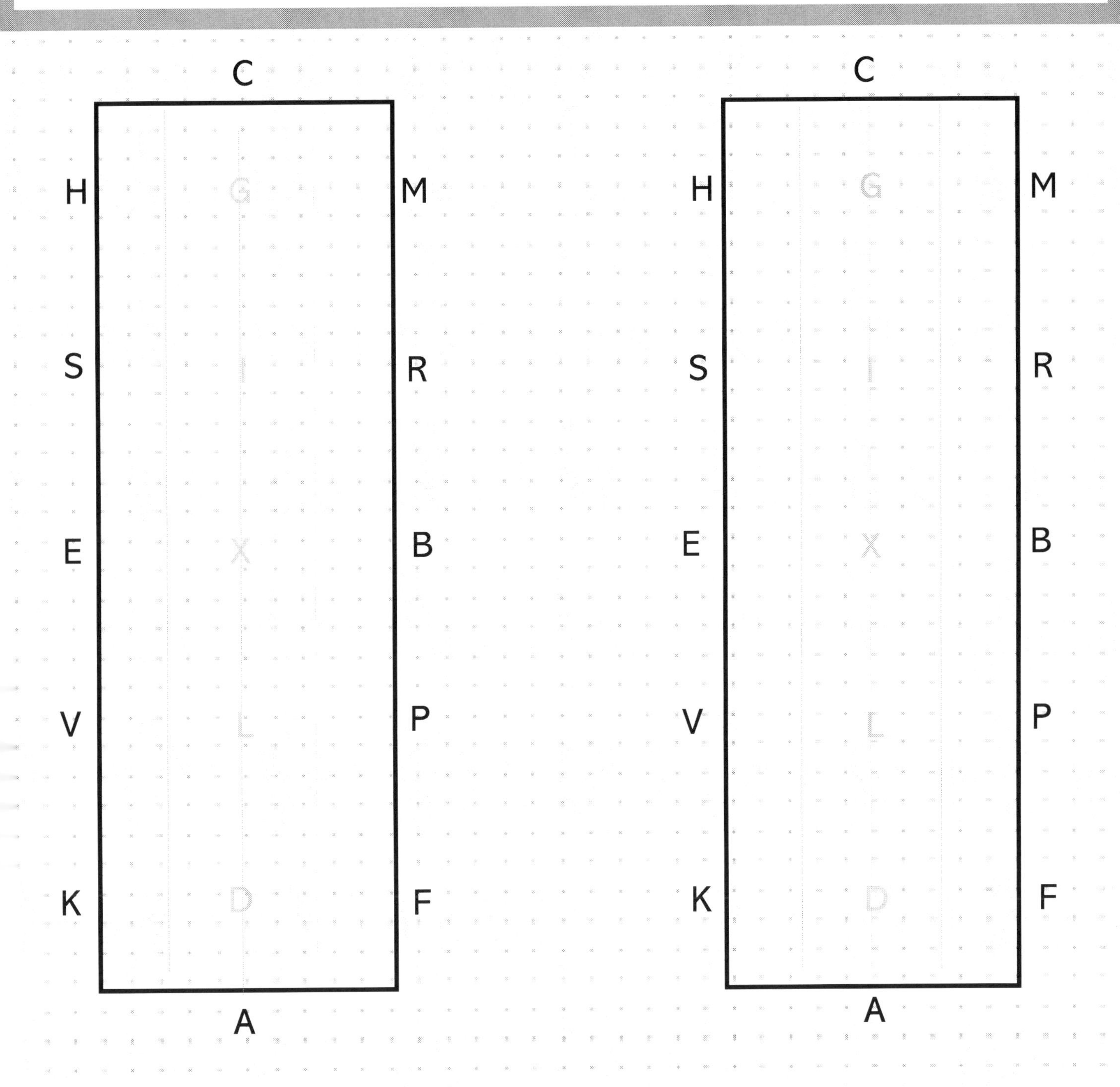

Notes:

Index

Topics	Pages

Index

Topics	Pages

Index

Topics	Pages

Index

Topics	Pages

I'm Stacie and I'm passionate about horses and learning. My career in horses began as a child and has included hunter/jumper, eventing, endurance, natural horsemanship and dressage. I've earned my USDF Bronze and Silver medals on my self-trained horses claiming state, regional and national honors along the way.

While working as a trainer and instructor, running my own stable, I was a classroom teacher in the middle school grades. Teaching well, guiding students through discovery, and embracing growth with fascination is my strength. I'm excited to offer unique tools and strategies to help riders accelerate their progress and reach their goals.

Stacie Campuzano

Manufactured by Amazon.ca
Bolton, ON